To Deland Sue

(Lord and Lady Lubash)

Best wishes

Eddie Lwern

WALK THIS WAY
Tales of a Tourist Guide

WALK THIS WAY

Tales of a Tourist Guide

EDWIN LERNER

BANK HOUSE BOOKS

First published 2005

ISBN 1-904408-15-X

© Edwin Lerner, 2005

Published by BANK HOUSE BOOKS

Printed and bound by Lightning Source

Designed and typeset in England by

BANK HOUSE BOOKS
PO Box 3
NEW ROMNEY TN29 9WJ

CONTENTS

To Larry

INTRODUCTION

Long before Monty Python or Fawlty Towers the comedian John Cleese used to do sketches for David Frost's television series The Frost Report. In one memorable solo piece, conducted as a monologue to camera, he conducted a three minute tour of Europe, acting as guide, tour director and general bully boy for a group of unseen tourists. As the impossibility of his task became clear, he degenerated into a raving maniac to great comic effect. It is one of the funniest things he has ever done, and you can see the seeds of Basil Fawlty, that other tyrant of modern British tourism, in the character he created.

Every guide and tour director will recognise Cleese's harassed and manic tour guide and most will laugh at it. This is no bad thing. A little healthy cynicism is useful in any profession to counteract pomposity and guides need it as much as anyone else. Civil servants laughed at Yes, Minister as much as anyone and office workers enjoyed The Office, while medicine has always been noted for its gallows humour. Anyone who cannot laugh at his job is probably not doing it properly.

Yet tourism is a seriously important business to Britain today providing us with around five per cent of Gross Domestic Product and over two million jobs. Tourist guiding is just one of these jobs, but for the tourist it is probably the most important. The modern coach tourist may not quite as harassed as Cleese's passengers, but they rarely have time to linger. They are moved from one impersonal space to another – aircraft or cruise liner to hotel room to coach to restaurant and back again.

Huddled in their tour groups they may have little contact with local people and maybe only a fleeting glimpse of local culture. During this time the one person they have a chance to interact with is their guide, who represents the human face of the country they are visiting. If the face is not a smiling one, if the guide does not seem to be enjoying his or her job, the memory of the country will inevitably be tinged with disappointment and anticlimax.

Guiding is a fairly new profession, having grown up in the post-war period starting with the Festival of Britain in 1951 (all guides love dates). Like many professions, it can take itself too seriously and become overburdened with considerations of qualifications and letters after names, factors which are of little consideration to the average tourist. Yet, the blue badge, the symbol of the professional guide, is respected not only within the industry but throughout the world and the methods used to train guides in London have been widely imitated.

Having gained a degree from Oxford and passed the Civil Service examinations, I applied for the guide course in the naïve assumption that it would be a breeze in comparison. I was soon disabused of this idea. A friend who qualified at around the same time said that the guide course was harder than the degree course, the implication being that a certain amount of elegant bluffing might get you through in academia, particularly in the arts, but not in this hotbed of competitive knowledge acquisition.

Twice a week we met at County Hall and studied London, its major churches, museums and historic sites. We learned how to conduct a tour of Westminster Abbey, St Paul's Cathedral, the Tower of London, British Museum and National Gallery. At the weekends we continued learning, practicing our skills in front of our fellow students on a coach taking in sites within reach of London such as Windsor Castle, Stonehenge, Bath, Stratford-upon-Avon and the universities of Oxford and Cambridge. Exam time in the spring saw us facing a panel of stony-faced professionals in the tourism industry, trying to impress them with our knowledge and delivery.

Then it was into the marketplace learning how to turn our hard won knowledge into a practical, interesting and entertaining tour. No, the average coach tourist was not that fascinated with the difference between early English gothic and perpendicular architecture, but did need to know where the nearest toilets were and how best to gain a good view of the Changing of the Guard through the crush of people there every day. We learned on the job how long people could concentrate on one topic, how far and how fast they could walk and how long they could last without what they euphemistically called a rest stop (a visit to the toilet) – around two hours, three at a push but not after breakfast.

After that it was on to the longer tours around Britain and Ireland, more training courses and a good deal of self-teaching as new cities and countries were explored. This was a new skill, that of tour directing, managing a group over an extended period, from a week to a month, developing skills that bring an often disparate group of people together, making sure that their suitcases and their elderly parents did not get lost en route. Some guides went on to taking tours around Europe and even farther afield, but I had neither the linguistic skill nor the desire to go beyond the British Isles for work. How else could you stand on the shores of Loch Ness, walk through the Shambles in York to the Minster, see a Shakespeare play at Stratford, drink the spa water at Bath (yuck) and cruise on Lake Windermere in one week?

Friends may think that it is all holiday, being a guide and tour director. The security of the monthly salary and the commuter journey is not for the guide, but rising at five in the morning in the cold and dark and making your way to meet a cruise ship or coach party that does not appear for hours is not always fun. There is plenty of work involved, some late nights and plenty of early mornings.

Highlights over the years include the views of two Australian ladies. One, standing at the viewpoint in the Trossachs on a beautiful August day with the heather in bloom around her, said that she now finally felt that she had seen the real Scotland. A month later, travelling over Rannoch Moor listening to a tape of Amazing Grace played on the bagpipes, another said that *this* was the real Scotland for her. The mist, the rain and the right music worked in that case. Another passenger, an American, more intellectually minded, said that being on the tour had been his best learning experience since his masters degree twenty years earlier.

Not many people come on a tour with quite such ambitious ideas, but the vast majority of people who do so enjoy the experience and many plan to repeat it if they have the time and money. One discerning and intelligent woman from the USA has travelled to Britain with the same company over sixty times since retirement and has enjoyed every tour she has done. Not all tourists are that keen. For many a tour is a quick survey that allows people to see the overall picture and travel independently in future. It is the modern way to travel - cheap, convenient and comprehensive.

Of course, sometimes it seems superficial to people outside – corny jokes, hectic schedules, too long on a cramped coach. Disillusion can spread to those on the inside. You look forward to the season ending when the clocks go back. There are fewer tourists in the winter, with a little surge around Christmas, and in the dark months of January and February most guides hibernate and some travel abroad. Then the spring comes around and the tourists return with the daffodils. It is time to go back on the road and make some more money, tell the same stories and jokes and maybe add a few new ones as well. This is also the time when new guides qualify and are met with both greetings and grimaces by their experienced colleagues (more bloody competition).

Tourism on a large scale is here to stay, at least as long as we can move people between and across continents. Some people will prefer independent travel, but most want a guide, an interpreter, explainer and, most of all, a human face to make their visit come alive. This is the story of those who have tried to do that.

A few technicalities

The problem with a book like this is how personal to make it. I have tried to say what I consider to be important about tourism today without being too academic. Obviously a good deal of it is based on personal experience as a registered guide and tour director over the last twenty years, but a series of personal anecdotes would soon become irritating. If you are looking for "Confessions of a Tourist Guide" please stop now. That book could be written but not by me. The first six chapters are a survey of incoming tourism and the role of the guide, while the later ones are more concerned with personal reflection on issues that I feel are important.

As is common in the informal business of tourism, I have used first names when referring to passengers or colleagues and have changed names to avoid any potential embarrassment – for them or for me.

'He or she?' There will never be a fully satisfactory solution as to whether to use 'he', 'she' or 'he/she' in the text. In fact, guides (and tourists) are slightly more likely to be female than male, although the opposite is true of tour directors (see chapter two for the distinction). My suggestion, for what it is worth, is that male writers should use the masculine pronoun, while female writers can stick to the feminine. That is the policy I have followed – even when 'she' is more likely to be accurate than 'he'.

And some thanks

I am grateful to all those who have taken an interest in this project and have helped me. In particular Sally Empson for letting me sit in on the guide course, Leena Hazeldene, Helen Clapp, the late and much mourned Katrine Prince and Jim Lindsay for enlightening me on the early days of tourism and Barry Le Jeune and his team of coaching enthusiasts for help on early coach tours. For chapter eight (on archaeology)

I am indebted to Mike Pitts and his lecture and book on what he calls Hengeworld (highly recommended for those who wish to read further in this subject) and the final line of the book is a shameless steal from (or homage to) Hugh Grant's best man speech in Four Weddings and a Funeral written by Richard Curtis.

Finally, my thanks to all the tourists who have accompanied me over the years. I may not remember all your names and faces, and I am more likely to do so I you have complained or criticised, but you have taught me much of what I have learned over the years.

Edwin Lerner

April 2004

FROM GRAND TOUR TO PACKAGE TOUR

A Short History of Tourist Guiding

Visit any country house in Britain today and you cans see the modern day tripper and package tourist admiring the spoils of the Grand Tour displayed on the walls. Young men of education and wealth were expected to further their education and experience of life through an extended tour of the major cultural centres of Europe. This was the eighteenth century equivalent of the gap year, a chance for young gentlemen to broaden their horizons overseas before the responsibilities of marriage, children and careers kicked in. It was also an opportunity for older gentlemen whose education exceeded their means to find useful and rewarding employment as their guides.

Most of the men who went on the Grand Tour had already studied at Oxford or Cambridge and were increasing their store of knowledge and experience in the places where their predominantly classical education was originally enacted. Just as a PhD student needs a supervisor, so a grand tourer needed someone to accompany and instruct him. He was known as a 'bear leader' and was often considered a figure of fun. The diarist Horace Walpole called them "absurd animals". Walpole, like many private travellers, considered himself above taking a guide, but his own tour was not an unqualified success. He had set off with his friend, the poet Thomas Gray, but the two men fell out and returned to England separately.

These early guides were often the equivalent of the gentlewomen who had fallen on hard times and acted as female companions to other unmarried or widowed women of better means. They were above menial work but, without a private income, needed to earn their keep and so buzzed around their richer charges, providing companionship and guidance. There must have been plenty of tensions as they tried to control their boisterous and often bored clients. Lord Byron painted a picture of a spoilt young aristocrat, a fussy older tutor and a lazy servant that brought the British into disrepute on the continent for boorish behaviour. They will recognise that description at most places where the England football team plays in a tournament.

Some of these tutors were happy to enjoy the life of a gentleman by proxy despite the occasional humiliation of being a kept man. Others moved on to greater things. The economist Adam Smith and the essayist Joseph Addison both did their stints as bear leaders before fame beckoned. This trend, of young men working as guides before moving on to greater fame, still continues. The actor Tom Conti and the broadcaster Peter Snow are recent examples.

The upheavals of the European wars that followed the French Revolution made the leisurely travel of the grand tour virtually impossible. Social changes started by the fall of the Bastille meant that travel could no longer be reserved for the few and wealthy. No-one would want to tour through a France in the grip of revolution or engaged in European war and post-Napoleonic Europe was subject to unrest and uprising every generation or so. Stable peaceful countries are where most of us like to travel, particularly if their currencies are weaker than ours, and the grand tour fell into decline as Britain became isolated from the continent and xenophobia increased.

Meanwhile nineteenth century Britain was starting to organise a domestic tourist trade. Thomas Cook, the epitome of Victorian self-improvement, began life as a wood-turner, moved into printing and missionary work and then organised the first publicly advertised package tour in 1841. This was a long way from the grand tour, being a train ride from Leicester to Loughborough and back again, costing just one shilling (five pence). It was different in character as well as duration - a strictly teetotal policy was enforced. They sang temperance songs on the journey and smashed beer bottles along the way.

Any beer bottles broken on a Thomas Cook holiday these days are probably smashed in the name of excess rather than abstinence. Cook's early successes led to him moving to London in 1864 and setting up with his son John the company that still bears his name. Cook became the Henry Ford of tourism. He made his fortune by taking a simple idea which would appeal to ordinary people and applied economy of scale and efficiency of production to make it accessible to them. Others have refined the product, found new specialist markets and destinations and tweaked ways of outdoing the opposition. But it was Cook who had the idea first and so, if you want someone to blame when you see a coach load of tourists pulling up at your favourite idyllic site, then Thomas Cook, that hard-working and sober Midlands Baptist is the face to fix on the dartboard. It is not hard to find: he is on every one of the world's best-selling travellers cheques.

Thomas Cook's success was related to the growth of railways in the mid nineteenth century, the preferred form of transport for the Victorian middle classes who could not afford carriages and were becoming aware of places to visit that were beyond walking distance. They flocked to the Crystal Palace in Hyde Park in 1851 to see Britain's first major tourist attraction, the Great Exhibition. This gave many people their first taste of travel outside their own community: around six million came to London to admire the achievements of Victorian Britain and its empire. This is still the highest proportion of the population to have visited a tourist attraction in Britain, the nearest modern equivalents being the Dome in 2001 and the Festival of Britain in 1951.

While the Great Exhibition introduced many Britons to the railways, the Festival held a century later brought them on to the tourist coaches and set tourist guiding up as a viable profession. The food and fuel rationed Britain of the immediate post war period was a different place to the confident and prosperous Victorian Britain, in the middle of a long period of relative peace. In 1951 motor cars were still rare and most journeys were made by bicycle or bus. Guided tours do not work on trains but the development of the internal combustion engine and the electric microphone combined to make it possible for a guide to talk to a large group of people on vehicle moving through the streets of London.

Many of those visiting Britain had helped to save it from the forces of fascism. US servicemen came back across the Atlantic with their wives and families on transatlantic liners like the Queen Elizabeth and Queen Mary, which they had sailed in during the war when their speed allowed them to outpace the submarines. The new tourists saw famous landmarks like the dome of St Paul's Cathedral and Big Ben from their coaches, even if much of the city around them was still rubble. Hitler had done London's new tourism industry a favour by telling his bombers not to aim at Parliament, St Paul's and the Tower, so confident was he of eventually taking possession of them.

As the guided tour became a feature of a visit to the capital, a corps of guides grew up to satisfy the demands of both the foreign and domestic tourist. The first guide's badges were awarded by the British Travel and Holiday Association, the forerunner of the British Tourist Authority. These were brown in colour, with a space for the name of the guide inserted on a carbon slip. Later came a red badge and finally the now almost universal blue badge with the name of the guide etched on it under an image of Tower Bridge.

The first guiding organisation was founded in 1950. This was The Guild of Guide Lecturers, now known as The Guild of Registered Tourist Guides, universally referred to simply as the Guild in tourist circles. It was begun by seven guides who met at the George Inn in Southwark and its emblem depicted London Pride, the small flower that grew on many of the bomb sites around London. The name was inspired by the trade guilds of medieval England, which combined the functions of trade union, professional association and friendly society.

Medieval guilds, or livery companies, maintained

16

professional standards and publicly disciplined tradesmen who did not meet the standards laid down by their guild. There are still around a hundred Guilds in London with their own halls and memberships engaged in educational and charity work. Some of them, such as the Cutlers, still have a role in maintaining professional standards in their field.

Guides will learn about these guilds in their training and will pick up a story or two about them to use on their tours. So, for example, a baker who sold bread in short weight could be expelled from his company and, as a closed shop operated, he would be unable to make a living. To be on the safe side most bakers threw an extra small loaf into the basket when people bought a dozen – hence the phrase 'baker's dozen' for thirteen. Another common phrase, 'at sixes and sevens', is also said to come from a long-running dispute between the Skinners and Merchant Tailors. The two companies could not agree on who should have precedence when the freemen of the city marched along in the annual parade of the Guilds. An unseemly and confusing tussle between the apprentices took place every year as they disputed the sixth and seventh berth until a medieval compromise led to them alternating positions six and seven from one year to the next.

There was a deliberate echo of medievalism in the Guild's choice of name. The Guild did (and still does) have charitable and educational functions, providing lectures and visits for practicing guides and support for retired ones. It also acts as a policing organisation trying to prevent the use of unqualified guides. However, its main role was that of a trade union, setting the fee that guides charged for their services and making it a condition of membership that this fee was charged by them. The original fee was a rather quaint three guineas a day. A guinea was an auctioneer's term, worth a pound and a shilling (£1:05p), in which the shilling was the middleman's commission of five per cent. Charging in guineas gave guides an air of respectability and gentility that harked back to an earlier era before concentration camps and massive bombing raids. Tourists were looking for this earlier era and were only too happy to employ a guide to help them find it. Thomas Cook and his successors realised that mass tourism relied on economy of scale and businesslike efficiency for tour operators to make a profit from their customers. The guide would be the human face of the country visited and if it was a retired colonel or matronly lady with a plumy accent, all the better.

They were not figures of fun, however, but independent qualified professionals. As the number of both guides and tourists grew, money increasingly became an issue. By the 1970s an increasing number of people regarded guiding as the main or only source of income with which to support their families. With a low pound, tourism seemed to be the one part of the British economy that was booming, so there was a demand for their services. Guide fees had fallen behind a rapidly increasing inflation rate, so a group of guides campaigned to bring about a significant increase in their fee. It was increased to £12 a day and has since risen steadily and now stands at around £150 in London for guiding in English, more for guiding in a foreign language. Fees outside London are considerably lower and less well-organised.

Guiding outside London was growing, but the chance of anyone making a living from it was considerably lower than in the capital. The blue badge became the accepted symbol of the qualified tourist guide after the Tourism Act of 1969, which also established the British Tourist Authority. It superseded the red badge which had authorised guiding throughout England, as far north as York, although not in Scotland, which has its own system. Tourist boards were set up in every part of Britain under the 1969 act and each had its own system of qualification and registration. Some of these were more thorough than others and, while it took the best part of a year to study for and pass the exams in London, a few weeks might do for one of the smaller tourist board areas, where there was a demand for the occasional walking tour and little else. In the early 1980s the snappily titled Joint Working Party for Tourist Guide Training was set up to try and unify standards of teaching for all tourist board areas with a core curriculum of knowledge that could be enhanced with local detail. It would take the best part of another twenty years before this was finally achieved.

Meanwhile money again reared its head in the late 1980s in a dispute with the government that would have repercussions on guiding that are still being felt today. The history of fee-setting in guiding could take a book in itself. Suffice to say that guides are paid on a daily or half-daily basis, the half day rate being two thirds of the full daily rate. The Guild set fees every year and members were expected to charge these fees to tour operators who booked their services, although this was more of an informal agreement than a strictly enforced policy. Some guides were prepared to work at below the rate set by the Guild, either through meekness or opportunism, a practice frowned upon or castigated by more militant guides.

The fee system had been generally accepted by both guides and tour companies for over thirty years when The Office of Fair Trading (OFT) deemed it anti-competitive in 1985. OFT saw its role as promoting competition and dismantling cartels and extended this to the work of the self-employed who were expected to compete against each other on the basis of price as well as quality. Obviously guides have always competed against each other for work, trying to impress their potential employers with their promptness, reliability and all the other aspects good guiding (see chapter three). Nevertheless, there was a sense of solidarity amongst most of them that you did not undercut colleagues by offering your services at a cheaper rate. There were exceptions to this – for those who accompanied extended tours around Britain and Ireland and for those who effectively had a full time job with one company – but most guides were freelancers who valued a fee system that was being attacked by the competitive ethos of Thatcherism.

Guides now had to decide whether to accept this legal

challenge to their fee system or to fight against it. A long and costly legal battle with OFT was not practicable for a small organisation with under a thousand members and limited resources, particularly as the prospects of success were slim. (Other professions had tried and failed to challenge the legality of similar OFT ruling in the courts.) Could unofficial fees passed around by word of mouth survive, with some help from the newly established booking agency Tour Guides Limited, or would the fee system crumble into a free for all in which operators played guides against each other, looking for the cheapest and most pliable ones available?

An eleventh hour cavalry rescue was offered by Britain's largest white collar trade union, MSF (now called Amicus) which offered an affiliation agreement to the Guild. In return for the Guild becoming a professionally independent sector of MSF, the union would guarantee that it would back the legal challenge to the fee system, all the way to the European Court if necessary. This kind of takeover of a smaller professional association was fairly common for large unions anxious to increase their membership, and thus their influence in government and the TUC. They offered the greater resources of a big union in exchange for a portion of the subscription fees of the association's membership. The larger union gains members, the smaller association gains clout.

Such a move had to be put to the membership of the Guild of guides, many of whom still identified with the character of the medieval trade guildsman rather than the modern militant trade unionist. Some indeed were probably still a little sniffy about giving up their guineas for pounds when invoicing tour companies. A long period of heated and often acrimonious debate took place and a ballot was held. Despite the prospect of preserving the fee system from government intervention, joining the comrades of a union affiliated to the TUC was too much for most Guild members. A large meeting of the Guild membership was held and the result of the vote was announced to a packed and unusually quiet gathering of guides. Guild members had voted by nearly two to one against affiliating to a trade union.

This, however, was not the end of the story. Some guides felt certain that informal networking would not preserve the fee system and went ahead with the process of attaching themselves to the union. In 1988 they formed the Association of Professional Tourist Guides specifically for the purpose of affiliation to MSF. This was no longer the world of the quasi-medieval Guild with its gothic lettered logo. Rather it was a world of acronyms – the Association is always known as APTG – of computer databases and of mission statements. APTG's is "To provide a voice for professional Blue Badge guides, to promote the Blue Badge and to uphold its high professional standard and to protect our membership through the expertise of the Amicus union". This is certainly thorough but it somehow lacks the conciseness of the Guild's old-fashioned Latin motto, 'Amare, Laudare, Mirare', to love, praise and honour.

Membership of both the Guild and APTG is now roughly equal with around four hundred and fifty guides in each, a few guides being members of both. The two organisations provide similar services to their members in the form of a monthly newsletter and information diary as well as lectures and visits in the quiet winter months. In fact, they are like a long-divorced couple, at first squabbling about everything and throwing acid at each other, later co-operating in some areas while agreeing to differ in others and finally developing a resigned friendship. Recently there has been talk of reconciliation and remarriage through the practical difficulties of amalgamating the two bodies would be considerable.

Both organisations also publish an annual fee schedule. The main upshot of the affiliation of APTG with MSF/Amicus was that the OFT backed down from a legal battle with white collar trade unionism and allowed the publication of minimum fees to continue, albeit with the proviso that these are not compulsory. APTG publishes fees which are updated (i.e. increased) every year and sent to tour operators about six months before they come into effect, on the 1st April of the following year. They can exhort their members to charge these fees but, in practice, would find it very difficult to expel those who do not do so from the union. As it was virtually unknown for guides to be expelled from the Guild for undercharging, the situation is little changed in practice from what it was before.

The Guild, faced with a haemorrhage of members who opted to join APTG, soon began again to set their own fees with permission from OFT, who had moved on to bigger fish. These are not compulsory but are 'recommended' to their members. So what is the distinction between fees that are unenforceable and those that are merely recommended? Very little in practice, although APTG's membership is certainly more proactive in bringing pressure on guides to observe its fee structure than the more gentlemanly Guild.

Broadly speaking, the fee system for guides is well established and accepted within the incoming tourism industry, although there is plenty of room for different interpretations of it. Most people realise that some kind of system is necessary. It helps operators to cost their tours in advance and enables working guides to maintain a reasonable income in a city with some of the highest property prices in the world. Nevertheless, there is at present an excessive supply of guides over the demand for their services and this inevitably has led to some guides selling their services more cheaply than others.

The guiding fee is the rock on which both the Guild and APTG were built, although it also led to the split between the two bodies. Guides can join either, both or neither organisation, although most working guides are members of one or the other. However, there are other organisations for guides. (You are never short of bodies looking for subscriptions if you are a guide.) The main one of these is The Institute of Tourist Guiding, sometimes known as ITG, an abbreviation it dislikes, preferring the more Kafkaesque moniker 'the Institute'. This owes its existence, not so much to government interference as to neglect.

Since the 1969 Tourism Act guides had been trained and examined by their local tourist boards. Those who passed their exams were registered by the board for a small annual fee and usually had their names and addresses included in a booklet issued by the board. After the dust had settled in the dispute between the guiding organisations and OFT, the London Tourist Board (LTB) decided that it did not have the resources or inclination to run a school for tourist guides and wanted to concentrate instead on attracting business to London in the shape of conferences and individual bookings. This, like the action on fees, was in line with the Thatcherite ethos in which public service organisations were expected to justify their existence by increasing the opportunities for private ones to flourish. It is in marked contrast to countries such as Israel where guides have to do a university level course just in order to qualify. The LTB course was not as academic as this but it was considered a sufficiently rigorous and professional training to be imitated in other parts of the world.

There was no problem finding guides who were willing and able to train new and aspiring members of their profession. It is a useful source of work and an interesting occupation during the quiet winter months and plenty of guides have found it both highly challenging and modestly remunerative to take part in the winter training courses. However, there was very little unity to these courses throughout the country. In London and Edinburgh the courses were professional, thorough and expensive. Outside these capital cities, standards of training varied from in-depth to cursory.

Following on from the initiatives in the 1980s, and as a direct result of LTB opting out of guide training, it was time for guides to take control of their own training and qualification. Over a period of five years Fiona Grant of

APTG and Tom Hooper of the Guild set up first The Tourist Guiding Foundation and then The Institute of Tourist Guiding. This culminated in a reception at the House of Commons with the Minister of Tourism and, once the Institute was up and running, the award of MBEs to Grant and Hooper. The aim of the Institute was to set a minimum standard for all blue badge guides in the England, Wales and Northern Ireland, Scotland and the Republic of Ireland having separate systems of their own. However, there are plenty of people who describe themselves as tourist guides who are not qualified with a blue badge and the Institute's constitution allowed them to join as either associates or affiliates depending on their level of qualification.

Because it is meant to be an all-embracing organisation for guides of various different types, qualified or not, professional or semi-professional, the Institute could not fulfil the trade union functions of the Guild and APTG. It is an umbrella organisation for guides, providing a degree of respectability and professionalism to a hitherto pretty heterogeneous group of talkers. However, inevitably there was to be some overlap in its functions with those of the London-based guide associations. The Institute has an educational programme similar to that of the Guild and APTG, albeit on a smaller scale. To justify its annual subscription fee of over £50 it also produces, in common with APTG and the Guild, an annual list of its members both on the web and in book form. These websites and booklets list the guides who are members together with their qualifications, languages, specialities and contact details.

Setting up websites is expensive and time-consuming and at present there are three separate ones for guides in Britain, one each for the Guild, APTG and Institute. There are also three published lists of guides sent to tour operators and other interested organisations, as well as two slightly different fee schedules. Certainly, no-one can accuse guides of keeping a low profile, although the newly qualified guide in London might feel that there is an over-abundance of guiding organisations seeking his subscription, particularly as there is also a scarcity of tourists willing to put up the funds that would pay these subscriptions. Sometimes it seems that the less work there is in guiding the more organisations spring up to look after guides.

For the subscription junkie, however, there is yet another organisation to join. This is The International Association of Tour Managers (IATM), founded in 1962 by a dozen tour managers who met in London to form their own organisation. Tour managing, or tour directing as it is often known, grew up as tourism expanded in the 1960s and 70s. It involves accompanying a group on an extended tour, normally of one to two weeks, around Britain, Ireland or Europe (or a combination of all three). The differences and similarities between guides and tour managers will be dealt with in the next chapter. Suffice to say that, while qualifications mark out the professional guide, a tour director is defined more by longevity. This is how he is assessed by IATM, who have retained the older title of tour manager rather than the nowadays more prevalent tour director. Their membership qualification is similar to that of the actors' union Equity. To join you have to have already shown that you are a practitioner - thus ensuring chicken and egg type difficulties for those looking for an opening into the business. Once you have been a tour director for two years you can wear a silver badge inscribed with the organisation's initials IATM and, after five years service, you can wear their gold badge. Although it has since moved into training, IATM was not envisaged as an educational body, more of a social club for practicing tour directors who work in a scattered and diffuse profession.

While guides might like to think of themselves as being next door to academics, many tour directors regard themselves as more akin to entrepreneurs. They are proud of their independence, although they are actually more likely to attach themselves to one operator than guides, who usually flit around fulfilling short term engagements. IATM has a big conference every year, generally held in a tourist resort in an interesting location. Although practical and educational issues are discussed at these get-togethers, they are more like a big end-of-season party than a series of seminars. Tour directors talk shop, moan about their problems and compare earnings over the season just passed.

Guides too have winter meetings - talks, lectures and visits organised by their associations and the Institute. There is a pan-European association of guiding organisations, FEG, and a World Federation of Tourist Guides who have winter conferences similar to IATM's. The cost of these is tax-deductible for self-employed people and they provide a useful social occasion for professionals who tend to work in isolation. Dealing with tourists can be a lonely job at times and guides and tour directors getting together inevitably want to let off steam. For sheer concentration of noise there is little to match a group of guides at one of these events exchanging gossip, anecdotes and complaints.

One of the things tour directors will complain about is local guides – and vice versa. Yet they have a good deal in common as professions and many people work in both fields. What do they have in common and what separates them? It is time to look at some of the different categories of people who work with tourists.

GUIDING LIGHTS

Different types of tourist guides and their roles

George Bernard Shaw once described the professions as a conspiracy against the common man. Tourist guides, who have moved from the position of educated servants to that of independent professionals, have constantly to be on their guard against taking themselves too seriously. Their journey might be compared to that of doctors, another profession which has worked hard to win respect. In her great Victorian novel Middlemarch George Eliot draws a picture of the aspiring and idealistic young doctor Lydgate who finds that his enthusiasm for his subject and his rather lofty manner are of no use when it comes to paying the bills and that, moreover, many of his patients do not regard his status as that of a gentleman. Many guides, who come into tourism full of enthusiasm for the history and culture of their country, will sympathise with Lydgate's resigned transformation from idealist to realist. Just as he started off with great knowledge of the human body, but little understanding of the workings of the everyday mind of his patients, so many guides start with great knowledge of the history and culture of their country but find out the hard way that they have to learn to deal with the everyday concerns of their tourists. Both professions combine the academic with the everyday and both sets of practitioners have established their status as qualified and independent. Yet both doctors and tourist guides rely for much of their success on the 'bedside manner' that wins the trust of their charges.

There are several titles used to describe people who look after and talk to tourists. Each one comes with baggage and may have a certain cachet or lack of it attached. This book is about all types of guiding so, for our purposes, anyone who looks after tourists and provides them with information is a guide. However, there are several different branches of the profession and it is worth distinguishing between the different roles of the following people – although there will be inevitably be a good deal of overlap between them.

- **Tourist guide**. This is often abbreviated to 'tour guide', a term which is American but is also used in Britain. Americans being so important to tourism, many of their expressions have crept into British use, although not all are abbreviations (transportation for transport, for example). A tourist guide may conduct the same tour all the time – on an open-top bus, for example, or through a stately home – and these guides, usually called line of route guides, will have little personal contact with their listeners.

- **Blue badge guide**. This is a more specific term and applies to a guide who has qualified for the work in a particular area and has the small blue and oval metal badge that is a sign of his professional qualification. A blue badge guide will be authorised to guide in a particular area (London and surroundings, for example) but not elsewhere. They are the only outsiders authorised to guide in certain places, such as Westminster Abbey and Windsor Castle. They are usually freelance and take jobs on an ad hoc basis from tour operators. In the London area most blue badgers are professional and expect to make some sort of living from the work Outside London and other capital cities there is less opportunity to make a living from guiding, no matter how well qualified you are.

- **Tour director**. May be referred to as a tour manager, although this phrase is less used now. A tour director is responsible for accompanying a group on an extended tour of a week or two, possibly longer. He will be expected to give a commentary and may conduct walking tours around some of the cities visited. He might have a blue badge, although this is not considered necessary, and he will probably work for only one, or possibly two, companies.

- **Long haul tour director**. Tours that go to ever more exotic locations are increasingly popular – China, the Far and Middle East, parts of Africa – and companies running these tours need tour directors who are prepared to travel for several weeks or even months at a time. There is no clear distinction between a normal tour director and a long haul one and some people like to conduct tours around Britain and/or Europe in the summer and elsewhere in the winter - although this involves being on the move almost permanently.

- **Driver-Guide.** As the name implies, a driver-guide operates as driver as well as guide. He will take a small party around on a tour in his own car or, occasionally, one that has been hired for him. Most driver guides have the blue badge qualification but some have a badge specifically designed for this kind of work, although this has now been phased out. Guiding of this type is more personal and can be tailored to the needs of the party or individual that hires the guide and car. It also requires a reliable car and expensive hire and reward insurance, similar to the type that taxi drivers have. A driver-guide should not be confused with a:

- **Driver-Courier**. This is a coach driver who also takes on some of the tasks of a tour director and guide. Few things make a guide more apoplectic than seeing a coach driver controlling his vehicle with a steering wheel in one hand and a microphone in the other. Although this is illegal the law is rarely enforced by the police, so companies unwilling to pay for a guide employ a coach driver to conduct their tours. These are usually companies specialising in tours for British people – overseas tourists generally expect to have a guide/tour director *and* a coach driver on their tours. All coach drivers need a special PCV (Passenger Carrying Vehicle) licence to operate vehicles with over twelve passengers. They do not need, and rarely possess, guiding qualifications.

- **Courier**. Never call a qualified guide a courier. They hate the term and virtually nobody working in incoming tourism refers to themselves as one. The term still persists in certain quarters, usually in companies that do not employ guides very often, but a courier is usually thought of as someone who works in a holiday resort organising excursions and accommodation. Some of them have been on the receiving end of poor publicity recently, but most do a difficult and demanding job conscientiously. Many move on to become guides or tour directors.

In practice, there is a good deal of overlap between these different branches of the same profession. Plenty of guides work as tour directors because they appreciate the better financial security that can come with this type of work. Some tour directors become sick of living out of a suitcase and take their guide exams so that they can work from home doing day trips. Unqualified guides work to gain their blue badge, which gives them greater freedom and kudos, while some people flit from one type of work to another depending on what is available.

The most important distinction is between guides and tour directors. The best way to express this is to say that guides have an *external* qualification while tour directors gain their status through their *internal* success with a group of people on a tour. Guides are independent practitioners qualified and hired for a specific purpose, with an in-depth knowledge of the area they guide in. Tour directors, on the other hand, have overall responsibility for the success or failure of an extended tour that covers more than one area. They cannot know all of these areas in the same depth as the local blue badge guides. They may not even have been to some of them before, but they are expected to take a group there, locate the hotel to be used and liase with a local guide.

What are the specific responsibilities of a tour director? He (in this case more probably male) has certain specific duties assigned to him by the company he works for. He first of all has to bring the group together. This may not be as easy as it sounds as it could encompass driving between several hotels and locating those passengers who are on the same tour. Just getting people into their seats can be complicated and fraught process. He has to see that people who are travelling together can sit together – not always possible if the coach is full – and that they can continue to sit together as the tour progresses. Again, this is not as simple as it sounds. The tour company will probably operate a seat rotation system which has to be established early on. Some passengers will want to sit at the front, some at the back and some wherever they feel like on the day. If the tour is a long one, the rotation system will operate differently to that of a short tour. The tour director needs to be firm, friendly and precise at the beginning of the tour. This first hour or two of a tour can be the most intensive period of work for him in the whole time he is with a group and is critical for establishing his relationship with them and a degree of friendly authority.

He also has to check the luggage, another apparently simple task fraught with difficulties. Tour companies generally allow each passenger one medium-sized suitcase and a reasonable amount of hand luggage. 'Reasonable' and 'medium', of course, are both open to interpretation, ranging from the minute to the massive. Whatever their size all pieces of luggage have to be listed, labelled and loaded before the tour can start.

Sometimes a passenger feels – not without

justification – that the tour director is more interested in their suitcases than in them at the start of a tour. Most directors like a few minutes when arriving at a pick-up hotel to check the cases in peace before addressing the passengers. They know that if a case is lost, damaged or left behind then they will be held responsible, so they need to concentrate on locating the correct pieces of luggage, particularly items of hand luggage that mysteriously appear from nowhere. Members of the group, however, are anxiously waiting to pose a host of questions which they want answered immediately. They may not have had contact with anyone who can answer their questions, so they swoop on the first person who looks like he knows his job. Checking luggage, answering questions, making people feel welcome and seeing that family groups sit close to each other: these are all part of the initial responsibility of someone taking an extended tour around Britain or the Europe. And often at six or seven in the morning.

At the end of the day, a tour director has to check a group into their next hotel. This, again, is a process which is easy to get wrong, but satisfying to get right. Most hotels do not require groups to register individually or else they allow them to do so at leisure, so the tour director can often just hand out the keys to his group and then take care of the luggage. Generally speaking, the faster the check-in is done the better, with the proviso that giving passengers the wrong kind of room only takes a moment, while changing them to the right type can take an hour. It is also an opportunity for a passenger on a coach tour to see some of the advantages of group travel. They may be vaguely aware that travelling in a tour group is somehow un-cool, that 'real' travellers go by themselves. If they can see those same travellers standing in line waiting for tickets or hotel rooms, and paying considerably more to do so, they will feel that the tour process is worthwhile. It is worth a tour director taking a few minutes to point out the advantages of their type of travel over that of the individual who has to do far more of his own legwork, the implication being that the director is taking out all the hassle and much of the expense of travelling, leaving just the pleasure for the tourist.

Does the lucky tourist actually have any responsibilities for the success of a tour or can he leave everything to the hard-working tour director? Well, yes. A selfish or greedy passenger can easily spoil a tour for other people, no matter how hard his director works. He must be made aware of his role in making the tour a success. Call them rules and regulations, if you like, but certain things must be firmly and clearly established to all passengers early in the tour. They basically can be boiled down to four things – rotation, smoking, attention and punctuality.

Rotation may sound childish (and may be dispensed with for certain groups who are used to travelling together) but it does ensure fairness for all on a tour and is generally accepted as the best way to organise seating. It is up to the director to organise the most appropriate system, using simple arithmetic to divide the number of days in the tour by the number of seats so that everyone has at least a chance to come to the front of the coach for a day of the tour. A simple system of labelling seats makes life easier for all concerned and saves arguments amongst passengers first thing in the morning. Seat rotation also has the not inconsiderable advantage of ensuring that the same passenger(s) does not sit just behind the driver and tour director for the entire duration of the tour, which can be a blessed relief for the professionals, if nobody else.

Smoking used to be allowed on tour coaches but is now almost universally banned. Coach operators dislike it because it makes the vehicles smelly and dirty; tour companies dislike it because most people are non-smokers; and most passengers have a very low toleration of even ancient traces of smoke. This is one of those areas where the differences between Britain and other countries is deplored rather than celebrated. Most English speaking tourists come from countries where toleration of smoking is much lower than it is in Britain, and it can be a major culture shock for tourists who choose to go into a quaint pub to find that there is a thick fog of smoke spoiling their evening or lunch break.

Tour directors may also have to become used to noisy and impatient demands for non-smoking hotel rooms and dining venues from people who are otherwise quiet and pliable. So low is the toleration of most tourists on coach tours for smoking that a company which advertised its tours as being completely non-smoking would probably steal a march on its rivals. There would, however, be problems in finding sufficient non-smoking hotel rooms for these clients and, at present, smokers are welcomed on tours but must accept the kind of restrictions imposed on them which they are probably quite used to at home. In fact, it is not an uncommon situation for a tour to be made up entirely of non-smokers – with the possible exception of the driver and guide. If this is the case the professionals are well advised to keep their smoking discreet or even secret. Coach drivers are not allowed by law to smoke while they drive.

This is probably the only legally enforceable ban on smoking amongst the range of prohibitions imposed by tour directors and tour companies. On the basis that one is allowed to do anything that is not positively prohibited by law, smoking is legal anywhere in Britain except where a bye-law or safety regulation prohibits it. As the law stands, a relatively small number of organisations have the legal power to ban smoking on their premises or vehicles and hotels and tour companies are not amongst these. Therefore, a tour director's ban on smoking on the tour coach probably has no legally binding force. This may be a nice academic debate for the lawyers but, in practical terms, a tour director should have the authority to protect the comfort and health of the majority of his passengers by banning smoking at least on the vehicle and by ensuring that dining and other communal areas used by the group are smoke free, as far as practicable.

In an interesting twist on the perennial smoking in public debate, Southern Ireland has recently banned smoking in all public places. The old drawback of taking people to a traditional pub there – the almost inevitable presence of cigarette smokers – has now disappeared. And with remarkably little protest. Ireland is truly changing and is now overtaking Britain in the fast lane to a new twenty first century ethos.

Attention is another area in which he needs to achieve a degree of unquestioned authority without being overbearing. Knowing how much to talk, when to say something and when to keep quiet - these are skills that guides and tour directors develop through experience. There are times when people, overloaded with cultural and historical information, just want to switch off as they snooze or gaze out of the window. It is easy to impose commentary on people in these situations and to work hard to nil or even negative effect. This is particularly a fault of guides who become tour directors – talking too much. (I should know, I was one of them.)

No tour guide or director can force his passengers to listen to him. He cannot make them take a test on what he has told them, although a voluntary quiz with a modest prize can be fun on a dull stretch of road. (It has the added effect of revealing just how much people have taken in.) A few people will be bored by the guide and there is little he can or should try to do about this – apart from making his commentary more interesting. However, most passengers take at least a passing interest in what they are being told and they expect information if they have paid for a guided tour. They expect to be able to listen to it, moreover, without having interruptions from other passengers talking to each other. It is not unreasonable, therefore, for the tour director to ensure that a commentary is audible and intelligible. There is nothing wrong with a post-lunch snooze on a coach (plenty of guides and tour directors have those) but there are few things more frustrating for passengers who are interested in a guided tour being unable to hear it because of the chatter of their fellow passengers.

Punctuality is one of those few more things - waiting for the latecomer. Now, this is what puts off many people from going on a tour, being unable to extend your free time to suit your own inclinations. Again, experienced guides and tour directors become used to gauging the right amount of time for most people at particular places, even though they will not always get it right for all passengers. At times it is necessary to have a word with a tour member who is consistently late as one person's persistent lateness undermines both the tour director's authority and the unity of the group, who resent being kept waiting by someone who is still taking photographs or shopping when others are ready to depart.

Sometimes the latecomer has just got lost. This can happen with elderly passengers and is particularly prevalent in older British cities that are not arranged in the logical grid pattern found in many towns in newer countries. The tour director gradually learns where such places are and who those passengers are who are likely to become disoriented. It is always a good idea to identify a prominent landmark and to repeat the time and place of the pick-up on several occasions in an attempt to avoid lateness before it happens.

As well as establishing rules and regulations, checking luggage and organising passenger seating, a tour director may have to arrange transfers, find a local doctor or hospital for sick tour members, convey news from home and even settle disputes amongst members of the tour group. He may well also have to sell and organise optional excursions. This could involve taking the group to a cabaret or entertainment show in the evening. Most tours are on the road well before office workers are at their desks, so the touring day often starts early and finishes late. With long periods of his life on the road, the tour director is not in a job that encourages stable relationships or predictable career patterns, although the financial and emotional rewards can be high when tours go well.

Life for the tourist guide who concentrates on day and half day tours is altogether more straightforward, although the problem can be one of boredom through repetition for those guides who do the same tour time after time. The way to move from this repetitive guiding is to gain guiding qualifications that allow a greater variety of work. Although standards vary throughout the country, the blue badge is the undisputed professional qualification for a guide. Training for blue badge guides is designed to provide a degree of versatility so that guides can pick up a variety of tours in their area and conduct them all with equal confidence. Because work in tourism does not fit neatly into the boundaries imposed by tourist boards, they are expected to be able to adapt themselves for work outside their area.

In London, which has the most difficult and expensive of the guide courses in England, it takes over a year to gain a blue badge, costs around £3000 and leaves those who pass the exams both exhausted and elated. Guides have a series of practical examinations that involve conducting a coach tour around London, guided tours of Westminster Abbey, St Paul's Cathedral, and the Tower of London as well as museums such as the National Gallery and British Museum. During these tests potential guides are told to take over the tour at random and talk to a group of stony faced professionals from various parts of the tourist business. They are expected to provide interesting and accurate commentary at all times and never dry up – even in a traffic jam.

They also have to take a set of written exams on the history of Britain, all the major sites within a day's drive of the capital – Windsor, Stonehenge, Stratford-upon-Avon and others – and aspects of Britain's cultural and contemporary life. Questions crop up on shopping, politics, sport and first aid and essays on history, archaeology and architecture are set in strict exam conditions. Many already well-qualified

37

people find the guide course and exams very challenging. No-one can bluff their way to the blue badge.

Tour directing, on the other hand, is full of bluffers. It is a curious wild west kind of a profession with virtually no formal qualifications, little training and none of the intellectual rigour applied to assessing guides. In fact, the contrast between the two could hardly be greater. This means that, although there is a good deal of interchange between the two jobs, the transition is not always a comfortable one. Tour directors, who may have little detailed knowledge of the areas they are taking parties to, may be asked awkward questions on subjects they do have not a clue about. They often have to fall back on a local guide's knowledge. Guides have a whole different culture to deal with when they become tour directors.

There is one area where conflict can arise between a guide and a tour director. This is when a qualified guide finds that that his duties are being performed by an unqualified tour director or even by a coach driver. This may happen on what is known as a panoramic or orientation tour, a drive around tour on a coach, usually lasting between one and three hours, in which the tourist has a chance to see the major sites of a city from a coach but does not go inside them. These are useful tours for people who have some free time in a city and who will use that time to visit places that they see from the coach, planning and paying for their own visits and organising their own priorities.

A good panoramic tour should highlight all the major places of interest in a city and help the tourist in this process of prioritisation. A guide in London, for example, might take the coach over Tower Bridge to get the best view of the Tower of London and tell passengers that they can see the crown jewels on display there as well as the place where Henry VIII had two of his wives imprisoned and executed. He might do well to mention that the Yeomen Warders at the Tower (commonly nicknamed beefeaters) do their own tours for the casual visitor and that it costs over £10 for a visit. He could provide similar information on Westminster Abbey, St Paul's Cathedral, the British Museum and National Gallery and even a few specialist sites such as the two Tate galleries, Madame Tussaud's Waxworks and the Globe Theatre.

Now most or all of this information can be imparted over the microphone by a reasonably sharp tour director or driver (although the driver would be breaking the law in talking whilst driving). To save money some tour operators will not hire a guide for a simple two hour panoramic tour but leave it to the tour director or driver to fulfil this function. This, not surprisingly, does not go down well with qualified guides, particularly as they have a pretty good idea that they (or one of their colleagues) supplied the unlicensed director/driver with much of this commentary in the first place. No guide goes through the long and expensive process of training in order to provide a free course in instant guiding to someone listening in and lifting their stories, jokes and information.

We see here a glimpse of the paranoia and insecurity that is meant to beset professional comedians, who regularly find their best material recycled by amateurs or rivals. However, there is no copyright on the spoken word and every joke, story and anecdote used in a guide's commentary is subject to reuse by anyone listening to it, be they tourist or professional. On occasions, a guide finds that a story he has honed to perfection is unusable because it has already been told to a group by someone who (he is sure) has not so much as reheated it as rehashed it, adding inaccuracies and embellishments that spoil the original point of the tale.

There have been attempts in some European countries to prevent unqualified people from overseas acting as guides. Some of these are semi-legal or illegal, ranging from dirty looks to tyre-slashing, while other places have legally enforceable codes. In Rome, for example, coach tours have to transfer their passengers not only into the care of a local guide but onto a local vehicle. In Britain the authorities show very little interest in the qualifications or competence of anyone holding a microphone on a coach, even if he is holding the steering wheel in the other hand. There have been attempts to privately prosecute coach drivers who act as guides but they have achieved little, apart from bad blood between the parties concerned.

European Union rules allow professionally qualified people to practice in another country for short periods as they become established and endeavour to gain local qualifications. These rules were somewhat absurdly going to apply to guides so that a person qualified to take you around Westminster Abbey would automatically be able to do the same in the cathedrals of Milan or Madrid. At the time of writing it seems that this has been discontinued and EU rules recognise that guiding is, in Euro speak, 'site specific', so that guides need knowledge of the particular place they are showing people around. This, however, does not apply to tour directors, who are a largely un-policed profession.

Where qualified guides have been able to protect their position is at those places where they have exclusive guiding rights, places such as Westminster Abbey, St Paul's Cathedral, the Tower of London or Windsor Castle. This is when local knowledge and training is vital not only in imparting information but in liasing with local site managers. They have to know not only the history of these buildings, but their geography as well. This includes the best order in which to see the places of interest, the entrances and exits (often different for groups and individuals) plus the all-important toilets. Guides are, or should be, aware of those rules and regulations which many sites, particularly churches, place importance on such as rules on dress code, photography (usually prohibited indoors) and respecting the pause for prayers that most churches have every hour.

Of course, there are times when unqualified group leaders take parties into buildings where they are supposed to have a guide. Some years ago I observed an American student group being taken into Westminster Abbey by their teacher. "Look, kids, Isaac Newton!" he said, as they walked down the nave towards the choir. A dozen flashbulbs went off before a surprisingly good-tempered Abbey marshal came over and told the group not to take pictures in the church – and to remove their hats (baseball caps, mostly). The point of this incident is that an unguided visit to Westminster Abbey is pointless for tour parties and for all but the best prepared individual. Not only were the students not told who Newton was and why he was buried there, but they were totally unaware of what sort of building they were in, that the Abbey is where the coronation takes place and that, as a result, it became our major national church and the burial place for many famous Britons. Any professional tour director would have known that a guide is needed for these things. There comes a limit to the extent that you can bluff your way with a group and that limit, in Britain at least, comes at the front door of places like Westminster Abbey and Windsor Castle.

There is also a limit to the extent that guides can expect to impose their hegemony on work in incoming tourism and this is at the front door of the tour coach. There is very little future in blue badge guides and their various organisations trying to make the police enforce rules on who can and cannot talk on the microphone in coaches going around Britain. This is not an area where there is a either a tradition or a perceived urgent need for legislation and, even when the law applies, as it does for coach drivers giving commentaries while driving, enforcement by the police is negligible. Large tour companies often have a series of early morning pick-ups at different hotels in London where tour directors will gradually assemble their parties. Inevitably they will talk to them on the microphone as they perform this process and point out places of interest as the move around. Some of these tour directors will be qualified as guides, while others will not. It is inconceivable that the Metropolitan Police would stop these coaches to check of the credentials of the tour directors while this process goes on during the beginning of the rush hour.

On the whole, however, guides and tour directors knock along reasonably well together, each knowing that there are certain areas where they have distinct and different responsibilities and that they can co-operate in the grey areas. One of the main reasons for this is that many people jump from one type of work to the other. Tour directors often sign up for Sally Empson's blue badge guide course on London and enter a structured environment in which they can, with hard work, gain enough knowledge to pass their exams and add, as they often put it, another string to their bow, even if it is one which they do not draw back very often.

Guides who wish to become tour directors, on the other hand, are usually thrown in at the deep end and left to sink or swim. I well remember my own experience of floundering and just managing to stay afloat when, as a blue badge guide with a couple of year's experience, I signed up for a season of extended tours around Britain. I soon found that those hard-earned qualifications meant nothing in the unforgiving world of tour-directing. Companies that employ large numbers of tour directors tend to use highly developed systems of client assessment. These subject the performance of the tour director and just about every other aspect of the tour to the grilling of customer satisfaction ratings. Clients are asked to fill in forms giving their opinion of the tour and the person who has conducted it. Not only is the tour director expected to get good personal ratings, he is expected to be an effective ambassador for the company. It is not much good for a tour director to be popular with his passengers if that popularity is not reflected in overall satisfaction with the tour.

Most American tourists will know that Harry Truman had a sign on his desk which said simply 'The buck stops here'. Tour directors would do well to carry one around with them and look at it each day to remind themselves of their responsibilities. These are wider than those of a guide, but not as deep. He may not know the difference between Norman and Gothic architecture but he had better be sure that all his clients' suitcases are accounted for and that those who want non-smoking rooms get them. The guide has the luxury of leaving those problems behind when he gets off the coach to go home.

CHAPTER THREE:

MAKING YOURSELF USEFUL
The Dos and Don'ts of Guiding

Each member of a profession experiences that uncomfortable but exhilarating shift in the transition from student to practitioner. Medical students start to deal with real blood as well as bloody-minded patients; lawyers exchange the seductively elegant complexities of legal argument for the need to present the self-justifying half-truths and distortions of damaged people to a cynical bench and a sceptical lay jury in the best possible light. Theory to practice: it is what makes grown-ups of us. Even the academic, who necessarily lives in a world of speculation rather than certainty, has to accommodate his teaching methods to surly and recalcitrant undergraduates. Many of them are very good at developing the kind of rhetorical tricks that guides use.

Nor would we have it any other way. We are all of us anxious to test our newly acquired skills on the wider world, to see which ones work and which do not. We develop ruthless and sometimes vicious defence systems of humour to remind us of those times when theory and reality are at odds. These become milestones in the path of maturity from eager and naïve student to detached professional.

As guiding is a profession that relies on communication, naiveté can be a positive virtue. Many guides look back on their early tours, when they were full of enthusiasm but empty of judgement, and are astonished that people seemed to enjoy what later seem like endless explanations of historical, architectural or archaeological data. They are then equally puzzled that, having mastered the art of judging how much information people can take in and how they like it presented, they find a group who do not respond to their well-rehearsed stories and carefully modulated explanations. How could they have liked that tour when I went on at such length about subjects they could not possibly be interested in, yet they did not respond with anything like that enthusiasm when I presented such a well-ordered tour to them, they ask.

What happened was that the first group was responding to the enthusiasm the guide showed in his early career rather than the experience he manifests later on. Tourism, like most human relations businesses, can be a hollow affair at times. People who are used to a comfortable environment and a slow pace of life find themselves being shifted from one soulless environment to another often at great speed and by those who are only too glad to see the back of them once they have paid their bill. While workers in hotels and restaurants know that repeat business is theoretically important to their employer, it has little practical application to them at the end of a long shift. In any case, they are unlikely to have much loyalty to these employers as they tend to work seasonally and casually for low wages.

So, when a tourist finds someone who actually seems to be enjoying their work and putting some effort into it, they respond in kind. Even the slowest individual commands a series of well-developed antennae that can distinguish enthusiasm that is genuine from that which is forced. Look at the faces of people in publicity photographs or chorus lines of long-running shows on the stage and you soon notice them tightening their face muscles to show their teeth under instruction or out of habit. While you can instruct your mouth muscles, it is much harder, virtually impossible, to bring the kind of light into your eyes which indicates enthusiasm for your subject and profession.

Guiding, therefore, is one of those jobs where, somewhat unfairly, new practitioners will sometimes have an edge over older ones. The light in their eyes is genuine, while that in the eyes of older guides may have faded or even disappeared. This is why some people qualify as guides, start working and then seem to fade away once the rush has worn off. They work for a season or two and then move on to something else once their energy level wanes, even though they can still run a perfectly competent tour. Their stars burn brightly but fade quickly. Yet other guides have stars that continue to glow steadily if not fiercely. They work year after year and retain high levels of both personal and customer satisfaction. They combine the two essentials of a long-standing guide – enthusiasm and experience. When there are tourists in town their telephone rings. How do they do it? How do you do it, if you want to become a guide? And what do you have to remember when you have become one, when you have studied yourself almost to death, have sat your exams and are sitting at home with your shiny blue badge waiting for the phone to ring? What are the secrets of getting the kind of feedback that ensures you will be remembered when the operators need a guide?

Of course, some things cannot be taught. Some people naturally have the kind of talent and personality that ensures they will be successful if they choose the right field to go into. These obnoxiously talented individuals need no guidance, only admiration - and envy. The rest of us have to learn, first in theory, then in practice. All you can hope to do is to add to your stock of theory, so that the transition to practice runs a little more smoothly.

Nor should an approach to work be too bound by any set of abstract rules. Guiding is a job which allows people to be themselves to a large extent. Trying to imitate other successful guides is probably not a good idea for a newcomer. Yet there are certain rules that should be obeyed and it is worth listing these, however obvious they may seem once set down on the page. This will have an impact on the amount of work guides are offered. The way they behave towards potential employers is usually a good indication of how they will behave towards that employer's clients. Being sycophantic can be as off-putting as being rude. It is a mistake to think that doing what the operator asks unquestioningly is always the right policy. Professional people always appreciate a thorough approach and being tipped off tactfully of potential embarrassments – when an attraction is closed, how long it will take to go from A to B, and what might appeal to a particular group – can be a good idea. Good operators always work with guides and tour directors and rely on their feedback, as well as that of the clients. At least the advice is free.

The qualities of a successful guide – as seen by those whom they work for and with – can be summed up in the word *professionalism*. Now this may not necessarily be an attractive word. It can evoke the image of a smooth operator, friendly on the surface, detached and cynical underneath, a phoney who has no commitment beyond his pay cheque. Of course, money is important to a professional guide. It is, after all, what distinguishes him from an amateur. Tour operators know that guides are not cheap but they do expect them to be value for money. They look on the professional guide as someone who can be relied on to bring their clients back well satisfied with the tour they have been on. Not, note, satisfied with the guide, but with the tour. The two are not necessarily the same. A guide represents the company he is working for and needs to bring about the possibility of repeat business.

So let us list what it is that a company look for in a guide. These qualities, in a very rough order of priority, are:

- Availability
- Reliability
- Loyalty
- Courtesy
- Humanity
- Humour/Informativeness
- Specialisation
- Appearance
- Price

Availability is obviously essential for a guide. Many freelance guides bemoan the fact that they have three empty weeks and are then suddenly offered work by two different people – on the same day. They cannot divide themselves in two and have to lose one of the jobs. There is nothing much they do can about this, but it is worth doing a little networking to try to prevent this happening too often. Letting operators know you are available/still alive – particularly if you have taken any kind of sabbatical – is worthwhile, if not easy. If the upside of being freelance is that you are no longer tyrannised by one employer, the inevitable downside is that you are ignored by many.

If more than one operator wants a particular guide's services on a given day, then it is quite common for guides to pass on work to colleagues. All blue badges in a particular area are considered to be of equal value and a guide might be in a better position to find a substitute for a particular type of job than a tour operator. In this case, it is necessary to clear such passing on of work with the operator concerned. Most operators are happy enough with the guide doing the legwork, but some may have distinct preferences and pecking orders of their own. It is better for the guide who turns down work to at least offer to pass on the job to a reliable colleague. If all goes well, he can expect to be called again in future if he covers a job he cannot do rather than if he simply refuses it.

However, having to turn down work is not necessarily a bad sign. It shows you are in demand. It can help to be proactive in advising tour operators of your availability, i.e. telling them when you are free in advance rather than waiting to be asked. Regular employers and guiding agencies, in particular, would expect this, while occasional or only potential employers might find it presumptuous. It is probably best to err on the side of presumption than modesty. The guide who is known to be free is more likely to receive a call than the one who has not made himself available.

Reliability (with its sister Punctuality) is the child of availability. Nothing is more infuriating for a tour operator than a guide who says he will be at Terminal Four, Heathrow at a quarter past six and does not arrive there until a quarter to seven. Sometimes this will not be noticed because of delays in the air, the runway or the customs hall, but the guide who makes a habit of cutting it fine will be caught out sooner or later. Lateness is more critical at certain times and places, the beginning of a tour and an airport being the most vulnerable points. You will find yourself struggling through the day or the week if you are not there when expected.

The shrewd guide will always be able to put himself in the place of the tourist. What will they think when they arrive in a strange country with no-one there to greet them? They are probably inexperienced and uncertain travellers, tired by the journey and confronted by language and currency problems. They need to be taken through the first hours quite carefully and sympathetically until they have found their feet. After all, the guide/tour director will need to ensure that the passengers are aware of the need for punctuality and he can hardly expect much loyalty to a code that he obviously not adhere to himself.

Loyalty may not come so easily to a freelance guide but it is critically important to a tour operator. Next time you go into a shop to ask for a particular item, check whether the person you are talking to uses the first person singular, the first person plural or the third person. If the assistant says, "I am afraid I cannot help you there," then you know that he is speaking personally and directly to you. He may be on an ego trip, but you might be able to appeal to his vanity for further help. If he says, "We do not seem to have that at the moment," you know that he is speaking with the voice of the company and that he will be able to help you as far as possible. If he says, "They don't stock that," then walk out of the shop straight away. "They" do not train their staff to identify with the establishment and are probably not worth bothering with.

The same applies to guides - although some might find the comparison with shop assistants unflattering. If (when) something goes wrong on a tour, it is very tempting to blame some unknown incompetent in the office, but this same incompetent may be paying the guide around £150 a day and expects a degree of loyalty for his money. If the guide identifies with the company he is working for, it increases the confidence of the passenger in both the company and the guide. If he distances himself from it, not only does this undermine the company, but it also undermines his own standing. He is regarded as merely a microphone holder, a story teller who has no real clout. Inclusiveness works both ways. If a tourist hears a guide say, "I will tell Charles about that," he knows that the guide not only cares, but that he has some pull and that he is worth listening to. Note the use of a name. The thought that someone in an office is going to take some notice of them, rather than simply cash their cheque, means people are more likely to write them in the future. If you do not know the name of the right someone, find it out. Or else make it up.

So, if an irate tourist yells at the guide, saying that "this whole tour is a shambles, the hotels are terrible, the coach is a disgrace and I want my money back!" how does a professional guide respond? He says (through clenched teeth) "Thank you for sharing that, Fred. We have obviously let you down and I appreciate that you are upset about it. Let us start again and see if we cannot put it right. It was good of you to let us know, so at least we don't make the same mistakes again." Or words to that effect.

Courtesy: Again, notice the use of the client's name in the response above. If Fred feels he is being treated as an individual with a point worth listening to, he is more likely to feel mollified by the reply and even to allow the hint of sarcasm implicit in such a saintly response to such a vigorous protest. He is also more likely to recall the whole experience in an amused way later on and to laugh about it with the guide. The curious thing is that people who express the greatest dissatisfaction can turn into the most loyal customers, far more so than those who do not give voice to or do not have discontents. There is a touch of egotism in this reaction, of course. Let a client tell you he is unhappy, convince him he is being listened to and that action will follow and you make a person feel part of the team and, as such, more valued than those who go with the flow. "They would be in a bit of state if I had not pitched in then," is how they feel.

Not everyone, however, will appreciate you using their name so freely. Habits vary with nationality. It is a particularly American habit to call people they have only known for a few minutes (or seconds) by their first name and this is a habit which has spread through the English speaking world, particularly in the business of travel and tourism, which prides itself on informality. This casual bonhomie is not universal and might be considered presumptuous in some European or eastern nationalities.

Humanity comes out of courtesy. It is the way that guides refer what they are talking about to the people they are talking to. You can be fascinated by history and archaeology and think that you are able to communicate this interest, but that will not necessarily make a tour come alive. People often need some point of reference that they can relate to for a tour to work. The occasional nugget of personal information, what Hollywood calls the back story, often supplies this. "I grew up in this part of the country and I remember this from my childhood," or "I used to work as an accountant/an actor/an actuary, so I know a little about this," are the kinds of sentence that people pick up on. They change the flow of a talk by moving away from the textbook to the personal, thus giving people something they would not hear elsewhere.

This can work in both directions. Change the point of view sometimes towards the listener. "Where are you folks from?" or, more specifically, "You are from Pittsburgh and will know all about coalmines, which Wales is famous for."

Again this will vary with nationality. British people on tour (and there are quite a few who take a tour of London on weekend theatre breaks) will have different interests to overseas tourists. A reader of the Daily Telegraph might be interested to hear that the daily column in his paper was called Peterborough for many years because the bishops of that city had their palace on the site of where the Telegraph's office in Fleet Street used to stand (the name has been moved to the Mail now). A driver of a Vauxhall car might like to know that the company's logo is a griffin because it was also the symbol of a man called Fulke, who lived where the company had its factory (Fulke Hall became Vauxhall). To take the story full circle, Fulke came originally from Luton, where Vauxhall cars are still made.

People from the USA, on the other hand, would usually like to see the American embassy in Grosvenor Square and would appreciate that the guide had thought it worth a detour to show it to them. On a longer tour an American party might like to see the village of Washington near Newcastle because that is where George Washington's family originated from. Their family coat of arms was a shield with three stripes and two stars, the inspiration for the original stars and stripes flag. It is almost impossible to fail to impress people if you personalise their tour in some way like this. They will see (and hear through the tone of your voice) that you are talking to *them* rather than to an unseen audience. Developing techniques of eye contact can make a huge difference to the way a guide operates as he realises what works and what does not.

By varying the tour to the group, the guide can avoid the aircrew syndrome. This is the epitome of repetition leading to boredom. Many airlines now use video installations to explain safety procedures but, when it is done by the chief steward over the aircraft PA system, it is almost a point of honour for seasoned air travellers to ignore the safety instructions while the cabin crew pirouette through the lifejacket demonstration. It is legally necessary for airlines to go through this procedure and the announcers must be discouraged from putting any individual variations into it. Inevitably monotony crept into their voices through repetition to the point where it seemed like a worthless exercise. Guides who have been doing the same tour for too long end up sounding like bored cabin announcers.

Humour: Humour on tours is dealt with in chapter seven. It is sufficient to say here that people remember if they laughed on a tour even if they do not remember much of the information. Guides, therefore, are famous for their reliance on a few well-honed and reliable jokes that resurface at the same time on every tour. For safety reasons it is not always possible to maintain eye contact with a group while on a coach. A guide may prefer or need to sit on a separate seat at the front of the vehicle without being able to see the faces of the people he is talking to. The easiest way to find out whether people are listening is to tell a joke and hear if they laugh. People who share a joke are brought closer by the experience, but there is no silence as deafening as that which follows a tasteless or badly told joke. Guides, therefore, tend to be very conservative when it comes to humour. Jokes, however, can have a limited shelf-life simply because the teller ceases to find them funny. He loses his sense of timing and the joke becomes lame and redundant. So he returns to reciting facts.

Informativeness: Information, of course, is what a tour is about. Inherent in the presentation of information is selection. A guide might use between a tenth and a half of what he knows about a particular site when telling people about it. Certain items of information are shunted aside and become effectively discarded through lack of use, while other ones are used occasionally for a particular situation – a group may be more curious than usual or have a specialist interest in a particular aspect of what they are seeing. While it can seem pointless learning information that will rarely if ever be used, it is good for a guide to know more than he needs. It gives him both the confidence and flexibility to vary his tour as circumstances demand. The good guide will always have something in reserve. A bad guide will always tell people everything he knows.

The balance between humour and information on a tour is the critical one. There are guides who can entertain their parties simply by telling long convoluted jokes, but they are few and far between and they can easily become tedious for the intelligent passenger. Generally speaking, most guides realise that humour is occasional while information is essential. If you just want jokes, buy a joke book. If you just want information, buy a guide book. Most people want both, but they particularly appreciate the balance between serious and light, and between the distant and the familiar that a good guide can give them. You can do a good guided tour without telling a single joke, but you cannot do one without giving information.

Specialisation comes fairly far down the list. This is not because there are not specialist groups who are looking for a guide, but because it is usually the group that is specialist rather than the guide. If it is an industrial or agricultural tour, the visitors will probably know all about alloy hinges or fat-levels in milk and will want to hear about other things that interest a group of typical professional people. If it is a sporting tour, they will almost certainly be both well-informed and partisan to boot. Many of these groups will take great delight in educating the guide about their specialisation – and how important it is in the scheme of things. A guide can always pick up a lot of useful extra information when doing specialist tours, which can then be recycled on an ordinary tour.

Having experience of a particular field can be useful in attracting work, but it is probably not critical - except in a tour which is advertised to members of the public as being particularly tailored to those with an interest in, say, the Beatles or Jack the Ripper. These will often be walking tours of a fairly short duration where the route is fixed and the chance to go into detail may be limited. Extended coach tours, however, can also be themed around a particular subject. Some guides have boosted their workload by being able to locate Platform nine and three quarters at King's Cross, or the locations used for Hogwart's School in tours that follow the Harry Potter trail (Alnwick Castle, Durham and Gloucester cathedrals and various parts of Oxford University). The latest craze across the Atlantic is seeing where Carrie and her friends discuss their sexual adventures in the series Sex and the City, although not many blue badge guides will gain work from that particular specialisation.

Language ability is a part of specialisation. However, being able to speak languages is not a prerequisite to becoming a guide in Britain. In fact, a large number of guides (including the author) are embarrassingly monolingual. This would be unthinkable anywhere other than in an English speaking country. Most guides in European cities would be able to conduct a tour in their native tongue, English and one or two other languages. The reason guides in Britain can get away with their linguistic ineptitude is simply because the majority of people coming to Britain are themselves English speaking. Not only do they want their tour in the English language, they want it from a native English speaker with a full command of the idiom and humour of the language. In other words, they want guides who speak English as their first language or who are effectively bilingual, so fluent in the language that they speak it like a native. In a non-English speaking country they would accept a guide with a foreign accent but not in Britain itself. For this reason Tour Guides Limited, the major guide booking agency in London, always gives priority to guides whose mother tongue is English if the group is also English speaking.

Guides who work in London in a foreign language are required to take a test by the registration authorities, originally the LTB, now the Institute of Tourist Guiding. These are rigorous tests and demand a degree of fluency that is close to being bilingual. Tour directors, on the other hand, will find having a smattering of a few languages very beneficial if they want to work in Europe. Many passengers come off European tours with stories of how their tour director could speak half a dozen languages. It is unlikely, however, that he would have enough fluency to conduct a tour in those languages. In fact, he might merely have enough phrases to be able to chew the ear off a recalcitrant porter or to communicate symptoms to a local doctor.

Guides can advertise their linguistic talents and will gain extra work from being able to take foreign tours around, particularly if they are familiar with or a native of the same country as their group. London's guides currently offer forty two languages, from Afrikaans to Welsh (although it is doubtful if there is much take-up for either of these languages). Most of these are European languages, although fewer people from Europe take guided tours than those from other parts of the world. The most desirable languages to speak for the purposes of gaining extra guiding work are oriental ones.

Having specialist knowledge is different to having a special interest or talent, a gimmick. Being able to recite some of the sonnets and speeches of Shakespeare is useful and can bring a tour of Stratford alive, but it is, in truth, unlikely to generate much work in itself. However, it is the kind of skill that adds to a guide's credibility and interest and makes him both remembered and employable.

Appearance: All guiding organisations emphasise the importance of appearance, far more so than the average tourist, who is dressed in jeans and trainers most of the time. Most of them are quite happy for a guide to be dressed casually but it sometimes helps to appear a little more formal than expected. It gives a guide a certain degree of authority and this can be useful, not only when talking to a group but when communicating with people from outside such as police officers, ticket sellers or hotel staff. A survey once found that men who asked strangers for money on the London Underground were four to five times more likely to succeed if they wore a tie. Many people come into guiding to escape from the tie-wearing environment but most operators will expect their guides to be at least reasonably smart. It is better to err on the side of conservatism than scruffiness.

Some guides have clothing gimmicks. Many male guides in Scotland wear the kilt (always the kilt, never a kilt). In England it is unlikely that many people would want to take a tour with someone dressed as a Morris dancer, but one male guide wears a bowler hat to great effect. Other guides have umbrella gimmicks, brightly coloured ones that are easy to see in a crowded area. It is important for a guide to be visible – popular tourist sites can be extremely crowded at peak times - but there is no need to look silly.

Price comes bottom of the list. This may seem surprising but, once an operator has made the decision to employ a guide, savings to be made by haggling over price are minimal. Of course, guide fees are far from negligible (particularly for the guide). Service tour companies that operate a large number of tours throughout the year, selling them directly to the public through brochures and agents, will employ a large number of guides and/or tour directors. The payroll costs of these people will be a significant proportion of their budget and they may attempt to save on this expense by tying guides into contracts that guarantee their availability. Some guides prefer to work like this and give up their freelance status to, in effect, have a full-time job as a guide or tour director with one operator.

However, many more guides are freelance and rely on work coming in from several sources. They invoice the operator after each tour is completed and fill in a self-employed tax return each year. The guiding associations set these fees to come into effect on April Fools day every year, the traditional start date for the tourist summer season. The London daily rate of around £150 may seem expensive to a cash-strapped tour operator, but works out at around three to five pounds per head for most groups, a significant but not crippling amount for the individual tourist. It is hardly excessive remuneration when one considers the average income for professional people in London, most of whom will have mortgages and families, but it can cause resentment amongst people with lower incomes in what is traditionally a poorly-paid industry with a good deal of price-related competition.

While most people honour the fee system, some guides feel they can gain an advantage by charging a lower fee than their colleagues. There is nothing to stop them doing this, although the professional associations of guides frown on the practice and would put more or less subtle pressure on them to either resign their membership or to charge the recommended fees. Undercutting, as it is commonly known, does happen, but it probably does the undercutter little good in the long term. Some tour operators will try to save a few pounds by offering a lower fee to a guide, but the guide puts himself in a vulnerable position if he accepts. The operator immediately knows that he can cancel the job at the last minute and delay payment for months if it suits him, secure in the knowledge that the guide will be unable to go to his professional association. He has undercut their fees and he has put himself outside their protection. In any relationship between an independent contractor and a potential purchaser of services, the contractor is vulnerable to the whims of the purchaser. He increases rather than decreases this vulnerability by acknowledging his weakness through allowing his price to be brought down. In other words, if you are prepared to work for peanuts, expect to be treated like a monkey.

CHAPTER FOUR:
TIME AND PLACE
Balancing the Two

Prioritisation is the modern buzzword. It does not even exist in the older dictionaries but is management speak for the process of determining how you spend your time and money. The government prioritises farmers, who are still heavily subsidised, over university students, who now have to pay their own way. The business person prioritises his big-spending customers over the ones who use up time without adding much to the bottom line. And the young tourist guide like me soon learns that it may be necessary to cut back the visit to Westminster Abbey a little in order to reach the Changing of the Guard ten minutes earlier. It will be busy there and the sooner you arrive the better for your party who will be anxious to take photographs before it is too crowded.

The guide as well as the tourist has to accept that there will *never* be enough time on a tour to see everything that can be seen, whether it lasts an hour or a month. There will always be someone who wants to spend longer at a particular place, there will always be another diversion you can take, another stop you can make. It is often the new guide, eager to show off his knowledge, naturally curious and full of enthusiasm, who spends too long at one of the early stops of the day and does not leave enough time at the last one, the one that people remember best because it was the most recent and the one they felt rushed through. That extra stop, that little diversion down a country road, that spontaneous idea which seemed so good at the time, does not work if it unbalances the day and means that a more important part of the tour suffers.

Balancing time and place: this is something that comes with experience. Planning is an important part of any tour, anticipating how long journeys take and how long people need before they want to get off the coach just to stretch and breathe in the open air. A simple photograph stop, for example, usually takes fifteen minutes in good weather. It can take five minutes for everyone to come off a full coach, another five to bring them back on and five to admire the view and take pictures. Four of these a day can take an hour off the last stop or delay your arrival at the hotel by the same amount of time, so a guide has to learn to be ruthless.

This is not to say that a little spontaneity is a bad idea. People appreciate a guide thinking on his feet and trying to add to the tour. Americans, who are big on these things, define different types of service. One speaker at a tourism seminar had a corny but oddly effective way of identifying the three kinds of service provided:

Downs stands for Doing it Our Way Negates Service. This is person who refuses to change the routine for any reason. The British equivalent is the Jobsworth, the man who always says, "It is more than my job is worth to change things for you."

Yes stands for 'You Expect Service' which is the basic standard but nothing more, while

Ups stands for Unexpected Pleasant Surprises, the little extras that make a tour memorable.

It might not win any Nobel prizes, but this is a handy set of acronyms to bear in mind. A few ups and not too many downs make a tour successful. It is the spontaneous acts, whether they are helping individuals to find a lost passport or stopping the coach for a photograph break at a particularly good spot, which make a tour work. Sometimes a guide can foster a sense of adventure by admitting he has not been to a place before and is particularly looking forward to seeing it, although the novelty of this can become wearing after a few wrong turns.

People appreciate when a tourist guide or tour director breaks his routine for them. However, there is a fine line between being spontaneous and being self-indulgent in guiding. In practice, most tourists do not complain about being given only a superficial picture of the place they are visiting. They are far more likely to feel overfed rather than undernourished when it comes to information. In fact, a typical tourist's complaint might be summed up as: 'Too much information – not enough time.'

What people want from their guide is some sense of the importance and value of where they are going. It is also vitally important that the guide shows them how to treat the places they are going to and through. The majority of tourists go a place once and do not return. They may have no knowledge of its financial state or of any conservation issues regarding it. They are, however, usually quite happy to obey the rules if these are made clear to them and most will cough up any money they are asked to pay in the way of donations to the fabric. The Institute of Tourist Guiding says in its Code of Conduct that "Members shall create awareness with clients and tour organisers/principals alike of environmental and conservation issues in order to avoid damage to any elements of the heritage within the area of qualification." In other words: don't spoil it for others.

That word heritage has finally appeared. It is in the name of the major conservation body English Heritage and appears in many discussions about tourism. For some the word is tainted with commercialism, the idea that the past can be exploited for money. The word is actually defined as "that which has been or may be inherited" by the Oxford dictionary. There is a sense in which our old churches and castles, not to mention the countryside, do not really belong to us but are kept for future generations. Guides rely on heritage for a living, so they need to be part of its conservation, if only to ensure that they have a chance of a decent pension. Does mass tourism aid or hinder the process of conservation? The overwhelming evidence is that it helps to preserve rather than destroy. Not only do tours bring money but they generally behave themselves. Of course, there will be times when unsupervised tourists run riot – almost always at times when they do not have a guide with them – and the sheer numbers of feet treading the same path can cause physical erosion in some sites. But if you believe that tourism destroys places, just take a look at Hadrian's Wall, or what is left of it. Many people come to Britain expecting to see something like the Great Wall of China stretching between Carlisle and Newcastle. What they see are a few scattered and ruined stretches of Roman wall a fraction of the size and magnificence of the original structure erected in the early second century AD. It was not modern tourism which destroyed Hadrian's barrier against the Scots and Picts, but medieval opportunism, people helping themselves to a readymade supply of building stone. This looting only came to a stop when the wall became part of our heritage.

Force of numbers has led to restrictions in popular places like Westminster Abbey, where the size of groups is limited to twenty six and at Stonehenge, where three quarters of a million visitors a year are allowed to walk around but not through the stone circle and must not touch the stones themselves. Likewise, in the Tower of London and Windsor Castle guides are allowed to walk their groups through the open air sections but have to leave them to go through the interior displays on their own. At places like Canterbury Cathedral and the Roman Baths in Bath, blue badge guides have to hand over to a local guide or, increasingly, instruct their groups in the use of automated sound guides. Guides occasionally moan at these restrictions and some have been known to try and subvert them. One guide took off his blue badge at Canterbury and even borrowed a camera while he walked through with his group so that he could guide there while pretending to be a tourist. (He has long since left the scene.)

Despite occasional and necessary restrictions, no heritage site in Britain wants to exclude tourist groups for the simple reason that they provide the bulk of a site's income. Only with money can conservation start and erosion be fought off. The downside of high numbers is easily counterbalanced by the upside of the income that comes with it and tourism is certainly a major source of income for both Britain as a whole and for individual sites.

Money, of course, is not everything and there will always be those who say that mass tourism destroys the very soul of a place, despite its financial benefits. There is something both impotent and irate about the way that people rail against modern tourism. These same sensitive souls hardly ever forego their own holidays in order to preserve the sanctity of the places they want to see. They merely complain about the extension of this right to the masses of humanity whom they want to be separated from. They are elitists, yet they would probably be in favour of causes like assisting public transport over the great car economy and they would be unlikely to argue against the right of others to vote in elections, for example. It is just in tourism that they are undemocratic.

There are two types of critics of mass tourism, the snob travellers and the nimbys. The snob traveller always puts himself above the package tourist and can be pretty much ignored by the guide, who will never satisfy him. Occasionally, however, the independent traveller latches onto the guided tour. This sometimes happens in churches like York Minster where there are a relatively small number of guided tours through a large building. You can almost see their thinking: "This fellow seems to know what he is talking about, let's listen in." This can be both annoying and flattering for the guide. It is best to ignore the freeloader unless he starts to impose himself on the group, at which point he must be politely ushered away. If this is done tactfully, there might even be a convert to the cause of guided tours.

The other anti-tourism type, however, needs to be treated with kid gloves. This is the nimby ('Not In My Back Yard') the one who does not want tourists anywhere near his place of work or home because they disturb his routine and his peace. Again, he is unlikely to be someone who does not travel himself, just one who lives in a place popular with tourists. He or she is normally someone who has moved to a particular spot without realising how popular it is with the outside world. Locals who have grown up with the presence of coach parties are usually only too happy to see one appear. They open gift shops and tea rooms to make money out of them and regard them as a good source of income. Forty or fifty middle-aged tourists can spend a lot of money in a little time and they will soon be gone to the next stop, unlike the backpacker who will hang around spending as little as possible without leaving a tip.

It is in the university towns that contrasts and possible tensions between the locals and the outsiders are most stark. People always want to see major seats of learning but the agendas of tourism and academia are very different. Tourists tend to be noisy, interested in the surface of things and in a hurry. Academics like quiet contemplation, looking beneath the surface and time to think. A tour might 'do' Oxford in an hour, while a scholar might spend a lifetime there without feeling he has fully understood what it has to offer. There is rarely open conflict between tour parties and colleges. Most of the porters at the front gates are quite welcoming provided the groups are well behaved. Guides have a major part to play in this, discreetly policing their groups so that they do not disrupt or disturb the life of the university. Cambridge has a more testy relationship with tourists, less used as it is to groups who visit and leave quickly on the way to Stratford. They have had too many French teenage groups brought unguided and poorly supervised to the town and left to roam, so that there are now more closed doors and forbidding looks than in the other place.

What will the tourists learn in their short time in Oxford? Ideally, they will know that it was not exactly founded but began to evolve around eight hundred years ago when a group of scholars set up an institution of learning on the banks of the Thames (known locally as the Isis) where oxen crossed over a ford in the river. The houses and halls used by these early scholars evolved into the modern Oxford colleges, each with its own tradition and character and around three to four hundred students apiece. They might find out the names and a little of the history of one of the colleges which they visit on their tour. Once all-male, the colleges are now virtually all mixed. If they come at examination or graduation time, they might see students wearing gowns, which reminds people that they used to live a semi-monastic life and were bound by the rules of celibacy that applied to all members of the pre-reformation church. This is why they acquire the title Bachelor of Arts on graduation (never Science, although that is also studied here).

The religious dimension of Oxford is critical to understanding the university. The tourists' landmark at Oxford is The Martyrs' Memorial and a guide might start his walking tour by describing how Cranmer, Latimer and Ridley went bravely to their deaths in defiance of Queen Mary's attempts to re impose Catholicism in England, although Crammer had tried in vain to buy his life by recanting his beliefs. The church is often thought of as a body that suppressed dissent and individuality. Indeed that great Oxford man John Wycliff was disinterred from his grave long after his death by order of the church to be swept unceremoniously into the River Swift for the crime of translating the Bible into English, long before William Tyndall was burnt at the stake for the same crime. Latin was the language of learning, English was for the illiterate masses who could not be trusted with directly reading the word of God. They would have to be content with seeing the pretty pictures in the stained glass windows of the churches they went to.

Yet the medieval church was not all about suppression. As barbarian hordes poured through Europe isolated religious communities kept a flame of learning and literacy alive. Would the Dark Ages have given way to the relative illumination of medieval times and then a brightening spread of literacy in the sixteenth and seventeenth centuries without the dedication of the early monks? Probably the best way to convey something of this combination of piety and learning is to point out the university motto, which is written on all those sweat shirts, calendars and postcards that tourists buy in Oxford: Dominus Illuminatio Mea – God is My Light.

A group might also be interested to hear something of the intellectual and sporting rivalry between Oxford and Cambridge (each known coyly as 'the other place' by its rival) as well as the differences between the two. There is more to this than just the annual boat race in March between Putney and Mortlake. There is a different feel to both places. While Oxford produces most of the great statesmen of Britain, ten times as many Prime Ministers as its rival, Cambridge nurtures more of the great scientists, not to mention the most notorious spies. If this strikes a chord, a guide might say that Oxford is more closely identified with the political establishment and even served as the royalist capital of England for Charles I during his war with Cromwell, who, like Milton, was in the more radical tradition of Cambridge. However, what the two universities have in common, represented by their joint name Oxbridge, is probably more important than what separates them.

Enough of history and structure. People will want to hear of some of the famous people who have studied and taught at Oxford, particularly the three great writers of fantasy: JRR Tolkien, creator of The Hobbit and Lord of the Rings, taught old English at New College (in fact over 600 years old) and is buried at Wolvercote cemetery; Charles Dodgson/Lewis Carroll, the shy mathematics don from Christchurch befriended and told stories to Alice Liddell, the daughter of his dean; and C S Lewis, who created the world of Narnia, spent many years at Magdalen College, was a friend of Tolkien and is remembered because Anthony Hopkins portrayed him in the film Shadowlands. Magdalen was also the college of the wit and playwright Oscar Wilde; Christopher Wren studied astronomy at Wadham College, before the Great Fire of London turned him into an architect and John Wesley virtually invented Methodism at Lincoln College. Margaret Roberts read biochemistry at Somerville and later became Mrs Thatcher at Wesley's Chapel in London; Tony Blair read law at St John's and Bill Clinton spent a year as a Rhodes Scholar at University College, to be followed there more recently by his daughter Chelsea.

These days, Harry Potter would excite more interest than most politicians. His creator J K Rowling has no known Oxford links, but his school Hogwarts was recreated on film at Christchurch and at the Bodleian library. If you visit Christchurch the head porter Tony Foxe will tell you how they used the stairway up to the hall for some scenes but that the building itself was too small (and probably too busy) for the film crew who copied and recreated it one and a half times its real size in a studio. Dodgson, whose portrait hangs in the hall, would be mentioned there but Henry VIII and Cardinal Wolsey's role in making Christchurch the largest of the colleges might be neglected in this story. They will return once Harry and Hogwarts have fallen out of fashion.

Is this superficial? Some guides might think it is too much for a short stop on the way to Stratford – and it is very unlikely that all these topics and people would be covered in one short visit – while those who live in and love the university would think it was just skimming the surface, that the great intellectual traditions and achievements of Oxford over eight centuries were afforded scant respect. A guided tour, however, is not a university course. There is, hopefully, a tip rather than a test at the end and a tour which flies over the head of those who have paid for it is of little use to anyone. Frankly, I would be happy enough if most members of a party of American high school kids on an Oxford and Stratford day tour from London, understood the motto on the sweatshirts they have bought and realised that the plays attributed to William Shakespeare were really written by the man from Stratford who married Anne Hathaway and not by Francis Bacon or the Earl of Oxford.

Some of them, devoted to their personal stereos, or making up for jet lag, will not even reach that far. Yet others will want to dig deeper and find out more than what they have skimmed over. Tourists are not homogenous and some are far more committed and curious than their fellow travellers. They also have priorities. Some places are bound to elicit more interest than others. A one week tour with three stops or more a day would cover around twenty to twenty five sites and it is unreasonable to expect that people will be equally enthusiastic about each one.

Many sites now use mechanical rather than human guides so that people can operate their own tours at a pace they choose. These devices, known as wands, look like large mobile telephones and provide taped information at different points of the tour. They are more reliable and ultimately cheaper than using line of route guides but they are not a threat to the livelihood of most professional guides, who simply introduce their passengers to them when they reach a site. How much they are used depends on the individual tourist, but it is rare for them to be listened to the whole way through.

A machine does not become hurt if it is switched off. The local guide or custodian at any site, however, is often less understanding. They have their own agenda for a group tour, which usually involves a far longer and more in-depth visit than the group has time for. The guide/tour director accompanying the group has to square this circle as he adjusts the time available up and the length of the tour down to reconcile the possible and the ideal. Some people can become quite huffy when their beloved church or country house is relegated to a lesser role than they consider it merits by a tour with a tight timetable. There is nothing like a tour director in a hurry to highlight your real place in the scheme of things.

Sometimes a guide causes problems for himself by being too generous, sometimes by being too greedy. New guides may take diversions or add in extra stops to go to some place that they are keen to see, leaving insufficient time at the last and possibly most important stop of the day, the one that people remember best. As experience grows, so too does the ability to timetable a day, knowing just how long it will take to get to one place or another and how long will be needed there to see it properly, if not thoroughly. This can vary from one time of the year to another, high season tours being noticeably more fraught and frantic than low season ones, when the queues are shorter. Hotels too vary in their welcome, shunting tours to worse rooms or booking them out when they have more high-paying private guests, who cannot barter down the prices in the way that tour companies can. No guide should underestimate the importance of the non-cultural parts of a tour in the scheme of things – ensuring that tourists get decent hotel rooms in overnight stops and that they arrive there in time to relax before any evening activity.

Most of all, they need to allow sufficient shopping time. Nothing irritates the average passenger more than an overlong tour conducted by a loquacious guide followed by a harassed tour director telling his people to come straight onto the coach as they are behind schedule. Never any time to shop – it is the kiss of death for a tour and for the guide. He may feel that he is saving people from the perils of commercialism but they will rarely thank him for it. When Westminster Abbey refused to allow groups of more than twenty six at a time, I occasionally had to split a larger group in two, leaving one half at the bookshop by the front entrance while the others went on tour, later returning to collect them while the first half used the bookstall at Poet's Corner. This complicated and unsatisfactory system, now discontinued, led on one occasion to a lady who had been on the first tour to complain to me that she had not had time in the "proper shop". The fact that she had had more time in the Abbey itself was of no consequence. The lack of opportunity to shop properly was her bugbear, not the lack of time to see.

Tourists always want to shop, to take away a piece of

what they seen with them. There is something primeval about this, making your mark on a particular spot and taking away a piece of it. This is why those who say that there is no point in going to places – you can see them just as well on photographs or television – are fundamentally wrong. There is a sense in which every tour is a conquest in miniature, the invader staking out a new piece of territory for his empire, or even an animal urinating to mark the boundary around his land. Souvenir acquisition is an important part of this process and should never be neglected.

Or overplayed. People do like to see things apart from souvenir shops on a tour. If they are constantly taken from one shop to another they inevitably question the motives of the person taking them there. Shopping is the add-on part of the tour, which follows on from the visit but does not act as a substitute for it.

The word souvenir actually comes from the French verb meaning to remember. The item may have little or no intrinsic value but it provides the key by which people unlock the experience afterwards. An important part of any experience is the reliving of it, telling your friends in the pub or over dinner. The souvenir is the evidence, the proof that the event actually occurred for the sceptical listener always on the lookout for invention or exaggeration. This does not have to be a particularly expensive or high quality item, a passport stamp or a label on the suitcase may be enough. In fact, sometimes the garish and obvious souvenir provides better proof than the finely honed item. This trend has now reached the stage that the souvenirs which sell best are those that boast how cheap they are. The one catchphrase to have impinged on most people from the world of tourism is: "My relative/friend/lover went to London and all I got was this lousy tee-shirt!"

No-one who buys these items does so because they will treasure them for the rest of their lives. They know they are buying rubbish and often joke about how it is made on the other side of the world in somewhere like Taiwan or

Hong Kong by someone who has never been near Britain or Ireland. It does not matter. In an experience that has few tangible rewards the souvenir is the reminder of the event, the key to remembrance. This is why tour companies hand out free bags, wallets and maps. If we are being literary they are the company's Proustian madeleines, items that recall the experience and remind people of the link with the operator. This, they hope, will bond the consumer with the company, reinforcing the relationship so that it continues in future.

Most of us, if we are honest, have some of these items in our homes. Amongst the treasured and handcrafted items are some trashy souvenirs that we are strangely reluctant to throw away long after their useful or their aesthetic life is over because they remind us of a trip we once took when we visited that church, that vineyard or factory. This has the curious effect that shops and stalls which sell cheap items reopen every year and do good business while the ones with pretensions to quality close down after a year or two, especially if they refuse to stock the tat that makes others prosper. These cheap and gaudy items are often stacked near the cash tills in shops so that, together with the cashmere sweater or silk scarf, a few key rings, pens and coasters find their way into the basket and onto the bill.

Of course, free souvenirs can be best of all. A guide can win friends with a little discreet pilfering of leaflets and maps that can be distributed amongst his passengers. These can be useful in preventing people from getting lost, but they also make handy keepsakes. Just make sure there is enough for everyone, or at least every couple, otherwise the effect will be to make some feel excluded from the giveaway. The giveaway is for the guide what the tipping system is for the tour operator – improving performance with no outlay. Free souvenir hunting can, however, get out of hand. Helping yourself to pieces of ancient monuments is not allowable. The guide must always remember that he has to return next year and needs to have something to show his next party. This is why the fences are up around Stonehenge: otherwise people would chip off pieces of the stones to take home. (A local ironmonger used to sell people hammers for that very purpose!)

The process of conquest by coach tour has to be thorough. A guide must always remember this when he is tempted to skip a stop that is on the itinerary, even if he thinks it will be a disappointment to his passengers. He should never fool around with the itinerary too much, excluding places which have been guaranteed by the tour operator, no matter how sensible this seems at the time. If something is expected it has to be included. It can be sensible to change the order of visits at times and, in case of an emergency like a breakdown, some particularly brutal prioritising will need to be done. However, the itinerary in the brochure is a contract between the tourist and the operator, in which the guide is an intermediary, an interpreter working out how it should be applied. If it says that they go to St Andrew's on their tour, they have to go there, even if the wind and rain off the North Sea make people want to get back onto the coach after five minutes.

St Andrew's is one of those stops that appeal to the non-tourist who buys a tour. An experienced professional can usually spot these people straight away. They are not interested in any of the historic sites, hate shopping, always want to come back to the coach early and go to the hotel as soon as possible. Yet there is one stop on the itinerary that persuaded them to come on the tour rather than to go fishing or hunting. This is often St Andrew's, a chilly town on the North Sea coast of Scotland about an hour and a half from the capital Edinburgh. It is not Scotland's oldest university, where Prince William studies, or the windswept ruins of Scotland's largest cathedral that attracts them. It is the thought that they might play a few shots on the world's oldest golf course.

The chances of anyone on a tour having a game of golf on the Old Course at St Andrew's are between slim and nonexistent. Such is demand for a round there that a complicated ritual of application and acceptance has to be gone through. As this involves staying overnight in St Andrew's, it is unlikely anyone based in nearby Edinburgh would be able to organise it, even with help from a guide. The golfer will have to be content with standing where Watson, Nicklaus or Woods won what they call *the* Open in the golfing world.

St Andrew's is a spot, like Hadrian's Wall, that looks more appetising on paper than in reality. A biting wind off the North Sea and a flat unappetising golf course are hardly likely to lift the soul at half past nine in the morning. Some golfers, used to carefully landscaped and well-tended courses, are disappointed in the Old Course at St Andrew's. It is not even technically a golf course at all, but a golf links, which is made from sand. The game of golf, a sport that demands more financial commitment from its players than almost any other, originated simply as a way for the locals to use some waste ground next to the sea. They had enough room to play nine holes out and then nine holes back and all major golf courses to this day have eighteen holes. Yet the guide cannot miss going there, even if the weather is foul. It is part of the empire being built by his party.

Tourism is the only empire in which the conquered welcome the conquerors. They sometimes do so with a grimace and they may say goodbye with a wave of relief, as the army departs with its spoils of souvenirs. Yet they would be worse off without them, not only financially. To paraphrase Oscar Wilde, there is only one thing worse than being overrun with tourists – and that is being ignored by them. A university, a golf course, a cathedral, even a beauty spot, can cope with properly policed and organised observers and visitors. Without them, they will die off.

This is unlikely to happen as long as we have the means to transport people in large numbers across and between continents. Whatever we think of it, mass tourism is here to stay. Another army will arrive next season and the one after that. The fact is that, despite overcrowding, hectic schedules and corny jokes, the great majority of people on a coach tour are well-satisfied by the experience and say that they would repeat it if they had a chance. Many return several times with the same company and even request the same guide or tour director, despite the fact that they know they will hear the same stories and jokes all over again.

Curiously, one of the best compliments a guide can be paid is for one of his clients to say that they cannot wait to get home – not to forget about what they have seen but to start reading up more about it, to rediscover some of the enthusiasms and interests that they had lost years ago. In the words of Philip Larkin's great poem Church Going, he hopes that someone will end up "surprising a hunger in himself". This is the best that a guide can achieve, to open a door. Whether the tourist enters it is up to him or her.

CHAPTER FIVE:

DRIVING YOU CRAZY
Relationships with coach drivers

The great majority of tours involve getting in and out of a large vehicle several times a day. Let us look at the vocabulary of these vehicles. They are usually called buses by the people who travel in them and coaches by the people who operate them. The difference is significant - but not critical: it is matter of status. A good tour driver would find it mildly insulting to be called a bus driver. He is in control of a coach, a vehicle that takes you on a tour in comfort, moves you at the most comfortable speed, slows down for places of interest and is always spotlessly clean. A bus is a means of getting from A to B. Coach journeys can vary depending on the nature of the tour, the preferences of the driver and guide, requests from the passengers or tour leaders, weather conditions, hotel changes and a multitude of other factors. Bus journeys, on the other hand, are regimented by advertised routes, stops and timetables, even if these are inevitably approximate.

Who is in charge of the route taken on a guided tour? This is a good question, not always easily resolved. It is worth looking at the relationship of the driver and guide because it is fundamental to the success of a tour. A good relationship – or one that at least appears to be good – is possibly the one thing that affects the tone of the tour more than anything else. A bad relationship between the two can poison the atmosphere and make a tour seem twice as long and half as much fun as it should be. The longer the tour the more important this relationship becomes – not least for the income of those who are working.

Many tours have a set route, which is fixed, like a bus route, to pass and possibly stop at several places en route. These may be advertised as being on a double-decker or open top 'bus' and are, in truth, often little more than bus journeys with a commentary. Most guides dislike them and find the lack of variety frustrating and ultimately soul-destroying. Turnover of guides on these tours is quite high as working on them involves repeating the same information over and over again to a sea of unenthusiastic faces. However, they fulfil a significant demand for those independent travellers who want to see the sights of a major city without signing up for a fully inclusive tour.

Those who sell and promote these tours have some of the worst reputations in tourism, accosting passers by with offers of a tour, sometimes fighting over potential passengers and clogging up the streets with sparsely populated and heavily polluting vehicles all on the same route. A tour like this has high fixed costs while the marginal costs of extra passengers is effectively zero, so they can only make a decent profit with a high loading. They end up giving not only tourism but free market capitalism a bad name.

Most guides prefer tours where there is a degree of flexibility. 'A half day tour of London' can cover a multitude of possible itineraries, from a purely panoramic tour on a coach past the main sights, to a visit to Westminster Abbey followed by the changing of the guard or St Paul's Cathedral and the Tower of London. Moreover, there are different routes that could be taken between these points with various possible stops for photographs along the way.

This is where the problems start. Differences between coach drivers and tourist guides can be exaggerated but they are real. Drivers tend to come from a different background to guides. Bluntly, drivers are more likely to be working class, guides middle class. Drivers have a job, guides a profession. Drivers work for money, guides work for – well, what do they work for? They do work for money, of course, for kudos, because they like to meet people, because they like to boss people around maybe. They may have a strong pedagogic impulse, which may just mean that they like to hear the sound of their own voice. Whatever their impulses, guides usually have a different agenda to drivers. They have a career to nurture and develop and need to return with satisfied customers, both for their own self-esteem and in order to keep the tour operator happy. Being self-employed they know that good feedback is important to their future in the business. A word from a satisfied group leader to a tour operator, a letter of praise from a passenger, just a round of applause can do wonders for a guide's morale and standing.

These factors have little influence on a driver. They are more likely to want a clean coach, a prompt finish and a trouble free tour. They are usually more concerned about police than passengers, about traffic jams and traffic wardens than scenic routes and photograph stops. The one factor that would endear a guide to them is the size of the tips they might get a share of. Tips, however, are unpredictable. Sometimes a seemingly bored group gives a handsome tip, while a satisfied or enthusiastic one might not bother at all. A round of applause is of little interest to a driver if it is not followed by a more substantial reward.

No-one can blame them for this. Drivers are employed, while guides are generally self-employed and their pay scales reflect this. On a full day tour of London the driver's weekly take home pay might not be much more than the guide's daily fee - and the day worked may well be longer for driver than for guide. The driver has to pick up his vehicle from a depot which is probably well out of the centre of the town. He will have to clean and fuel it when the passengers are away and he may face a long drive back home after the tour is over. Drivers face long hours for little pay and are expected to manoeuvre a forty foot vehicle through heavy traffic and narrow streets. When the journey takes the tour along a stretch of motorway or empty road, the only person on board who must never fall asleep is the one behind the wheel.

The driver is also far more bound by official regulations than the guide. While certain sites like Westminster Abbey will not allow unqualified guides, guiding as a whole is relatively un-policed in this country.

Drivers, on the other hand, are constantly in danger of being penalised for just doing their job. A few well-publicised traffic accidents involving coaches have resulted in coach drivers being subject to a raft of restrictive legislation that many feel threatens the very nature of their job. These are under constant review and each revision of the traffic regulation involves a tightening rather than a loosening of the restrictions.

Drivers must never drive more than ten hours a day. They need to take a day off every week or three days off after twelve days work; they must take a forty five minute break every four and a half hours; and they must have at least a nine hour overnight break from one day to the next. These restrictions may seem reasonable – and certainly some form of control of driving hours is necessary – but they can cause great problems for companies conducting extended tours, particularly in remote locations, where getting hold of relief drivers can be a real problem.

Most guides and tourists like to have the same driver as much as possible. Even if he is a difficult driver, you get used to his ways and can adjust to them. When a new driver comes in for a day or days, you have to become used to how he operates. The 'old' driver may need to find alternative accommodation and, if the tour is on the move, he may have to drive a car to the next hotel – even though he is not allowed to drive the coach there!

Driving regulations are not a primary concern of the guide, although he must be aware of them when he schedules stops, so that the driver can have a sufficient break. This is rarely a problem in practice, as people usually want more time than they have been given. (Any tour which did not stop for forty five minutes at least twice a day would have few repeat customers.) However, occasionally the guide or tour director will want to have an early start or push on to a particular destination, while the driver will refuse on the grounds that "I need my forty five minutes - or my nine hours" before the wheels move.

Strictly speaking the driver is not even allowed onto the vehicle during these break periods, so processes like loading luggage and even opening the doors for passengers have to be performed during working rather than rest periods. Theoretically, if the driver needs a break during a particular time because he has been stuck in a traffic jam, he has to stop the vehicle, go outside and wait for break period to pass – in the pouring rain, if necessary – before moving on. The guide and passengers are not subject to these rules and can wait in the dry interior while the driver is soaked outside - obviously a major contribution to road safety.

In practice, this would not happen because of the presence of the tachograph, a machine that sits behind the speedometer. This device records the time when the vehicle is moving, when it is at rest and what speed it travels at. (Coaches have a sixty two mile/one hundred kilometre per hour speed limit throughout Europe.) What it cannot do is say where the driver is at any particular time and, if he chooses to take his break inside his vehicle rather outside it, no-one will be able to tell just by inspecting the white tachograph cards that record each day's driving history. The police and Ministry of Transport inspectors can demand to see the previous week's cards at any time and, if the speed travelled was too high or the rest breaks too short, the driver can be fined and, ultimately, banned for repeated offences. Furthermore, coach drivers are just as vulnerable to speed cameras and spot checks as other drivers. A lost licence inevitably means a lost livelihood, so it is hardly surprising that most coach drivers show a degree of care over this issue when looking at the programme for the working day.

To a stressed out guide this degree of care can seem like paranoia or just sheer bloody-mindedness on the part of an awkward driver. However, the guide is not vulnerable to the fines and sanctions that a driver faces and must give priority to obeying the law. He does not face a long period out of work if the law is broken, so he has to bear in mind the responsibilities of the man who does. A little simple planning and consultation should iron out these difficulties in advance, so occasionally asking the driver "Do you need forty five minutes here, Ron?", shows that the guide is thinking of the position of the man behind the wheel. In practice, the driver is far less likely to demand a break if he is offered one than if he is not.

What the driving regulations have contributed to is a gradual undermining of the position of the coach driver. In the early days of guided tours in Britain, the same driver and guide would operate as a team throughout a tour. Often the driver would have more experience than his guide and would provide invaluable advice and help. This still happens, of course, but there has been a subtle shift in the relative positions of driver and guide in recent years. With the influence of legislation on the driver's role, they do not carry quite the authority they once had. In the last twenty or thirty years, guides have organised their profession and gone from strength to strength while tour directors conducting extended tours have been given more and more responsibility by the companies that employ them. At the same time the influence and authority of drivers seems to have slipped.

There are still a large number of coach drivers, however, who do not want a guide anywhere near their coach, except on a few occasions when they are allowed on to work strictly within the parameters laid down by the drivers themselves. These are on tours where the driver not only drives but acts as tour director, luggage loader and general top dog of the tour. Several coach companies organise their own tours and leave the driver to run the show largely by himself without the extra expense of hiring a guide. Some of these drivers are regarded as semi-legendary figures operating their own fiefdoms with impunity. However, they are not above the law. Not only does this restrict their driving hours, but it makes it illegal for a coach driver to speak on a microphone whilst driving his vehicle. While the first type of law, concerning driving hours, is enforced quite rigidly, the second type, banning talking on the microphone, is largely ignored.

Companies which aimed to attract overseas tourists to Britain and Ireland used to save on fixed costs by employing these driver-couriers to run the tour. However, the responsibilities involved in running an extended tour for overseas tourists – looking for lost luggage or lost passports, organising excursions, conducting walking tours – are so great that it is not feasible to leave it to one person. They soon realised that the tours worked much better if they employed a separate driver and tour director with distinct responsibilities and in Britain virtually none of the companies selling tour packages overseas still uses driver-couriers. In Ireland, where the distances travelled are smaller and the driving regulations are, ahem, less strictly enforced, the driver-courier survives on some overseas tours. In Britain the concept of one man doing both jobs only survives in the British market, i.e. pensioners taking their annual trip to Scotland or to the seaside are quite happy to have their Dave or their Jim to look after them. Homer and Ethel coming from the states are looking for something more.

Once the larger tour companies decided that the roles of driver and director/guide had to be split, many of the men who used to run their own tours as driver-couriers for Homer and Ethel had to choose between staying behind the wheel and holding the microphone. Most chose the latter, realising that the financial rewards and job satisfaction were probably higher in tour directing than in coach driving. Some chose to remain as drivers and had to face the prospect of being told what to do by a new tour director or guide who they considered to be wet behind the ears. One can imagine what was (and is) said about guides and tour directors by drivers who get together to compare notes: much the same as is said by guides comparing drivers.

Obviously there are plenty of opportunities for drivers and guides to clash in the running of a tour – driving hours, rest periods, start time, finish time, pick up and drop off points, how long is spent in a particular place, even what is said over the microphone. Plenty of drivers – who would not dream of allowing the guide to tell them what gear they should be in – are only too happy to add their contribution to the commentary. This can be very irritating for a guide who may be developing a riff along certain lines and does not want irrelevant interjections from behind the wheel. Sometimes, of course, it can be useful and interesting. No guide should ever stop learning and there is no reason why he should not learn from a driver as much as anyone else.

Drivers' contributions should, however, be treated with scepticism. A guide should always check if the driver says that a particular place is closed (he should check anyway). Occasionally, drivers have their own agenda and, instead of asking to run the tour in a particular order, pretends that it is necessary to do so. One driver insisted every time he did a Bath and Stonehenge day tour that "the stones are being cleaned this morning, so we have to go to Bath first". That has a certain bizarre creativity to it, but it is hardly convincing. In fact, watching the cleaning of the stones at Stonehenge would be not only unique but worth making a detour for.

Another contribution that proved completely bogus was the Elton John house. On Windsor day tours driver after driver pointed out to me a white house by the roundabout on the road between the castle and Runnymede, saying that was where the famous singer lived. I used to faithfully reproduce this comment, to oohs and aahs from the passengers who had heard of him, until a guide with a lot more experience and sense pshawed the idea: "As if Elton John, with all his money, would live in a house next to a roundabout." You see how these urban (or in this case suburban) myths grow up. It was known that Elton John lived near Windsor, the house looked fairly big and was easily seen from the route used and someone jumped to a conclusion which soon passed from guide to driver to guide and became established as fact. Guides have to go through the kind of intellectual training that is, in truth, far more comprehensive than they need for the vast majority of the tours they conduct, but which should stop them from repeating nonsense like this. Drivers have no such training and one wonders how many other myths have done the rounds since Elton's roundabout house.

Of course, drivers have other qualifications for their job. No-one can drive a coach with fare-paying passengers unless he has a Passenger Carrying Vehicle Licence (PCV). This was originally called a PSV for Public Service Vehicle and is different from a lorry driver's licence, which is known as an HGV (Heavy Goods Vehicle). One of the essential differences is that coach/bus drivers carry passengers, while lorry drivers carry freight, and there are certain safety and public service aspects of their work which they must be familiar with. Unless he has a valid PCV licence a guide cannot legally drive the coach in the case of an emergency and he would be well-advised not to try it. Modern coaches are usually forty feet (twelve metres) long and ten to twelve feet high.

Drivers also have to have health checks periodically to see that they are fit enough to drive. Having heart problems or diabetes can disqualify someone from driving and drivers are advised to watch their weight and smoking (although the advice is often ignored). These periodic health checks are considered as essential as the tachograph checks by the Ministry of Transport, which is always inclined to tighten the regulations when a well-publicised coach crash occurs, even if it is the fault of an over-tired or unhealthy car driver, who is not subject to the same legislation.

There have been suggestions that guides should have periodic checks on their intellectual rather than their physical abilities and that they should be retested every few years to make sure that they are up to speed. The Institute of Tourist Guiding was keen on this concept when it was first formed, but the idea did not progress. The marketplace does a good deal of weeding out of guides who have passed their sell-by date and guides are now left to organise and record their own continuing development. Drivers, on the other hand, need to be checked to see that they are not liable to a sudden heart attack while transporting forty to fifty people along a busy road. Physical health checks for drivers are considered compulsory, while intellectual recharging for guides is optional. This may seem uneven but is probably an accurate reflection of the priorities of both professions. Drivers are in a life-threatening position while guides are in a life-enhancing profession.

For this reason, guides should always remember that tourists must have confidence in the person behind the wheel. A poor driver threatens their actual safety whereas a poor guide who bores them to death will only do so metaphorically. This is a deep-seated psychological need and a guide ignores it at his peril. Anything which undermines their belief in the driver also undermines their feelings of benevolence towards the whole experience. This includes the attitude of the guide, who can do a great deal to improve the confidence of passengers in the driver's ability.

This need to believe in the man in control is one of the reason airlines and other transport agencies give quasi military uniforms to their staff. A pilot could just as easily fly a plane in jeans as in a gold-braided outfit, but the passengers would not have as much faith in him. Likewise the great majority of coach drivers wear a tie when driving and many have company blazers, even epaulettes to increase their authority. Frank Abgnale understood this when he conned his way into pilots uniform in order to cash phoney cheques. (His exploits were portrayed by Leonardo Di Caprio in Catch Me If You Can.)

This is also why, if there is an obvious conflict between the driver and the guide, the passengers will *always* side with the driver. Their lives are in his hands and they need to believe in the one turning the wheel, rather than the one holding the microphone. Only walking tours can operate without a qualified driver and they can rarely cover enough ground in the limited time available to the modern tourist.

So, if as occasionally happens, the driver and vehicle do not show up or they break down, the tour is effectively grounded and cannot go forward. In this case it is up to the guide or tour director to find a replacement driver and vehicle. Sometimes this just means making a phone call to the coach operator who will send out reinforcements. At other times, it means finding a copy of the local Yellow Pages and working through the coach and taxi companies until one is found which has a vehicle(s) available. The guide should agree responsibility for payment in advance in such cases. An outfit that uses vehicles which are liable to break down might not be financially viable enough to cover any extra expenses and a guide should *never* make payments to coach companies (or hotels) on faith and then hope to be reimbursed.

Up to this point the guide may seem like a peripheral figure on a tour. This is when his importance becomes clear. What vehicle is used is of little importance as long as it can transport the group and their luggage to the next hotel or back to base. If we are being honest, one driver is much like another when it comes to this basic process and obtaining an old school bus is far better than leaving people stranded somewhere. It also makes clear to passengers where responsibilities lie. If there is a breakdown the driver's responsibility is to supervise repairs to the vehicle and return it to the operator and, possibly, to the tour when it is fixed. The guide's responsibility is to see that the party reaches its next destination and that they then pick up the tour as best they can under the circumstances.

The guide stays with the group, while the driver stays with the vehicle. This illustrates the difference in their respective roles. The driver is essential but the guide is critical. The driver is needed more than the guide, yet the guide makes a bigger impression than the driver and is ultimately more important to the success of a tour. He is also the one who is held responsible for its success – or its failure. It is no excuse, if a tour goes badly, for a guide to blame the driver. It is the guide's responsibility to control the tour and work with the driver. While a good driver can help a guide a great deal, there comes a time in the career of every guide and tour director when it is necessary to face down a difficult driver and let him know who is really in charge.

Drivers can undermine a tour in several ways. Problems include being over familiar with the passengers. This ranges from merely talking while driving, which can be annoying, to full-blown sexual harassment, which can result in litigation. Being unfamiliar with a new route is not a major offence. Pretending to know where you are going and then getting lost is. While it is pleasing to have a competent and experienced driver, a willing newcomer can be just as good. A driver who thinks he knows it all but has no loyalty to the tour is the worst sort.

Perhaps the best way to look at the relationship between a driver and a guide is to describe it in terms of an arranged marriage. In some cultures bride and groom do not meet until their wedding day. The match is made from the outside and they are expected to make it work. From being strangers one minute they are expected to spend hours in each other's company and eat two or three meals together each day. The relationship works best if both parties are clear what role they are expected to play and where their responsibilities lie – breadwinner, homemaker, wheel turner, talker, whatever. The relationship founders when the parties are not agreed on their respective roles and each tries to do the other's job. (All analogies break down eventually: drivers and guides do not generally go so far as sharing the same bedroom, certainly not the same bed.)

This is not all one-way traffic. Drivers have every right to stand up to tyrannical or unreasonable guides. Just as a soldier is not obliged to obey an order that is contrary to international law, so a driver is not obliged to turn past a no entry sign or work beyond his legal limits. Interestingly, it is former drivers who have become guides/tour directors who are often most critical of the current drivers they have to work with. They sometimes find it difficult to leave the old job alone and try to do both driving and guiding. Just as a driver should never pick up the microphone, so a guide should never turn the wheel. It undermines the driver's position if it seems that anyone can do his job.

Whatever problems or difficulties guides and drivers have with each other, the golden rule is that they should be sorted out in private. Passengers should have no knowledge of what has gone on if there is a disagreement. This is natural self-preservation for a guide, who has a duty to back up his driver even if he finds him a pain in the neck. Again, the parallel with a marriage springs to mind. Once a couple start arguing in public and do not care who sees the cracks in their relationship, it becomes that much harder to cover them up. While guides and drivers can usually sort out their problems with each other on a one to one basis, if a driver is a serious liability on a long tour, it may have be necessary to replace him. If this is necessary – for example if he has a problem with drinking – the guide must be ruthless. Some short term ruthlessness may be needed for long term gain. The first the passengers should know of this is when they see a new face behind the wheel and find that the previous driver's wife/mother/dog is seriously ill at home which, regretfully, means he had to leave the tour suddenly. Until that time, the guide should encourage the belief that the man behind the wheel is the best there is. His passengers will probably think so anyway.

CHAPTER SIX:

A GOOD TIP

Pros and cons of tipping

People are always interested in money. It is something for a guide to talk about on one of those dead stretches, where there is nothing much to point out but the group looks as though it might appreciate some general information. They are interested in average income levels and tax rates, currently around £500 a week and ten, twenty two and forty per cent respectively. They are also interested in the National Health Service ("socialised medicine" is the rather distrustful American version) which people pay towards through their National Insurance contributions. There is even a certain amount of mileage in the difference between self-employed taxation, which allows certain business expenses to be offset against earnings, and pay as you earn tax, where tax is deducted from salary or wages at source. Almost all guides will pay tax as self-employed workers, so it is in their own interests to learn their way around the system.

On a more obvious level, tourists are always handling currency so it is necessary to know something about how the coins and notes are decorated. The Royal Mint print a handy leaflet explaining the symbols and mottos on the pound coins, which are worth getting to know: *Decus et Tutamen*, for example, is from Vergil's Aeneid and means "an ornament and a safeguard", while *Pleidiol wyf I'm gwlad* on the Welsh coin means "True I am to my country". The Scots don't waste time with such subtleties: *Nemo me impune lacessit*, written on the edge of their pound coins, is an ancient greeting from the Gorbals, meaning roughly "No-one disses me without getting their teeth kicked in – Jimmy". (Boy, you can really bore people at parties when you become a tour guide.)

Even the least involved people usually perk up a little when you start talking about what the average person earns and how much house prices are. "What do these run at?" is quite a common question when you are driving through suburbia. It is American for, "How much do these houses cost?" Likewise, "What do you make?" means "How much do you earn?" rather "What do you construct?" Americans can be quite abrupt about asking questions like these. The smart answer is, "Well, that depends on you." In other words, the more you tip, the more I earn. If asked, I say that I make a living - but not a fortune - from working in tourism.

However, plenty of guides struggle to make a living, let alone a fortune, particularly if they have qualified in the last ten years. If you are thinking of becoming a guide, the advice given to all trainees recently has been, "Don't give up the day job!" Guiding is predominantly a freelance occupation and there is virtually no job security in the profession. Most tour operators run small companies with unpredictable turnover and low profit margins and are not able to guarantee guides any kind of regular work. Some guides and, particularly, tour directors have reasonably secure contracts with larger companies that need a corps of people willing and able to work a whole summer season with the occasional winter tour thrown in. These professionals are the ones who come closest to job security, but even they find that the supply of work dries up very quickly if bookings are down or their performance is found wanting. The variation in income between the top and bottom of this profession is huge. Some people do well from tourism, while others do it on a purely voluntary basis because they enjoy it. Likewise, some people pick up a guitar or join an amateur dramatic company with only the idlest dreams of being discovered and whisked off to instant fame. There is not much fame in guiding but there are certain gratifications.

Is there a career in it? Well, not in the sense of there being a career structure, starting from the bottom and working up to a position of seniority. As we have seen in chapter two, new guides can make their mark quite quickly and sometimes edge out their senior colleagues through enthusiasm and novelty, although the extent of this can easily be exaggerated by disgruntled senior guides. Most freelance guides have an alternative source of income or else regard guiding as an occasional occupation to be combined with homemaking. This sounds like they are housewives working for pin money and that may be the case in some towns and rural areas, where guiding work is even more sporadic. However, with the present London rate of a hundred and fifty pounds a day, you can buy a lot of pins for a few days work.

You can, however, rarely pin guides down to a precise figure for their annual earnings. This is partly through coyness but also because work is so uncertain. Variables like currency fluctuations and international tensions have a huge effect on work prospects and, at the time of writing, there are signs that levels of work are finally increasing after several years of decline caused by fear of terrorism and a weak American dollar.

The one thing that guides were always able to count on was the dollar bill. It might not be worth much these days but there were usually a few to be had at the end of the tour from grateful American passengers who appreciated the guide's attempts to make the tour more interesting and a little more fun. Tipping for people from across the Atlantic is perfectly natural and not considered patronising. The guide should be ready for it at the end of the tour without assuming that it would come. He should always be there to say goodbye to his passengers when the tour is over and, if they choose to thank him with money, he should be able to accept that with gratitude but not obsequiousness.

Yet tipping can be a source of embarrassment and resentment on both sides of the transaction. Some people are against it in principle and others feel obliged to tip even if they are unhappy with the standards of care and service they have received. Drivers might depend on tips that the guide effectively earns for them, and they may be prepared to put pressure on people in the form of soliciting for tips, pressure that makes guides squirm with awkwardness. How can you tiptoe through this minefield?

First, let us look at the word itself. A popular but probably mythical etymology has the word originating as an acronym for the phrase "to insure promptness" as applied to coffee house waiters who were given a financial incentive to bring their drinks swiftly to the customer while they were still hot. More probably, it came from the idea that a tip was a monetary offering given as a form of bonus for good service to supplement the wages of the person being rewarded, the tip of the iceberg as it were.

The Oxford dictionary has a dozen definitions of the word tip. Ah, here is the one we want: "A small (?) present of money given to an inferior (??); a gratuity, a douceur" (sweetener). This makes a guide seem like a mere porter or skivvy who should be eternally grateful for any loose change that happens to tumble out of his master's pocket. Yet, the organisations that guides form when they get together use words like professional, registered and qualified in their titles to enhance the status of their members. In fact, many guides are only too anxious to assert their intellectual superiority over their clients. Maybe that is why they earn small tips.

Small might be a way of saying paltry, or it might be in comparison to the upfront earnings a guide expects in the way of a fee. However, not all guides earn big fees and, for many of them, tips represent a significant proportion of their income. Bad tips might come from a dissatisfied group or from one that has been ill-prepared by their tour director in the matter of tipping. The tour director will himself hope for a decent tip at the end of his stint of duty and he is well-advised to encourage people in his group to give a decent tip to a city guide – if they think he is worth it.

This is the crux of the matter. Some companies give guidance to their customers on tipping, but they usually add a rider along the lines of "if you are satisfied with the service you have received". It costs a company nothing to add these exhortations to their brochures and it makes them feel that they are entitled to pay their guides less than the full freelance rate for the tour because those guides will be earning generous tips if they do a good job and bring back satisfied customers. On the face of it, tipping is a godsend to tour operators: performance-related pay which has no impact on payroll costs.

However, some people come from non-tipping cultures and others have a non-tipping attitude. One lady on a three week tour, who had seemed very happy, surreptitiously slipped me a twenty dollar bill at the end of the tour apologising for her husband "who did not believe in tipping". Whether it was meanness or principle that persuaded him of the evils of this system was unclear – he saved money either way. Such passengers do appear occasionally, although few are so stuck on their principles that they refuse to give any kind of reward to a guide if they have had a good tour.

There is something particularly irritating for the low paid worker about the wealthy man who refuses to tip out of principle. Someone dining in a restaurant who earns £50,000 a year will probably be served by a waiter who earns a tenth of that before tips. Whatever the rights and wrongs of the system the eater has a clear duty to pay the waiter for his work. To misquote the poet Hilaire Belloc, it is the duty of the wealthy man to provide an income for the artisan.

What are the rights and wrongs of tipping? On the plus side it keeps people on their toes – boring guides and surly waiters do not get tips – and this helps to weed out people who are not suited for the job or whose attitude needs improving. It is a real pleasure for a guide or driver to be able to look at their tips at the end of the tour and have a solid reminder of the fact that they have done their job well. This is the performance-related aspect of tipping which gives the system its justification and its importance should never be underestimated. Despite all their qualifications and knowledge, some guides are simply not good communicators and do not have the right manner to deal with flesh and blood human beings. It is a mercy for them and their charges if they remain un-tipped.

On the negative side, it can encourage ingratiating behaviour that is irritating and embarrassing and which gets in the way of real communication. However, anyone with any sense soon realises that obsequiousness can be just as irritating as surliness, that David Copperfield sought out the company of the charming but arrogant Steerforth and avoided that of the slimy Uriah Heep. In the Middle East, for example, there is something refreshing about going to Israel, where people tend to be abrupt, sometimes positively rude, to tourists, in contrast to the nearby countries, where the arriving traveller is soon surrounded by hordes of people offering a hotel room, a meal, a girl, drugs for money, baksheesh as it is known there.

Possibly because of this kind of irritating and persistent servility, tipping seems to be in retreat in many modern countries, apart from the USA, where it still thrives. It is illegal in Singapore and not customary in Australia (two increasingly important sources of tourists) and, although people from these countries usually do their duty, as they see it, they would not be regarded as high rollers in the way that Americans can be. Some tourists would definitely prefer the guide and driver to be paid in full in the way that a service charge is often included in the bill in a restaurant, but major tour operators are unlikely to adopt that policy because it would only add to their upfront costs in a very competitive market. As long as the present system persists, most people will tip more or less willingly if they are happy with the tour.

But guides have to accept that some people simply do not tip. They devise code names for such people. 'Runners' is a favourite and, for a time, 'elbows' was another term, particularly amongst coach drivers. Having a sore elbow meant that you had experienced a very unprofitable tour, and to be labelled 'an elbow guide' by your driver was the kiss of death.

Sometimes a bad tip becomes a self-fulfilling prophesy. If the coach is cold, the windows are dirty and the driver is curt, he can hardly blame the guide for an unprofitable tour – although that rarely prevents him from doing so. Drivers can help themselves and their guide by looking after their vehicle and by helping to foster a good atmosphere. They are traditionally entitled to half the tip, although many people tip driver and guide separately. The guide has a responsibility to make sure that, if there is a tip or tips, the driver gets his share one way or another.

Yet, sometimes with a good driver, an entertaining guide and a tour that runs smoothly, some people do not tip well or at all when they say goodbye. They may be unhappy, they might be miserly, they might be broke, they might be against tipping in principle or they might be ignorant of the custom. The guide can only ever do anything about the first and last reasons – the first by making their tour light and accessible enough to be enjoyable, and the last by gently guiding their charges in the process of tipping.

This process is fraught with difficulties. Some guides on line of route tours have a habit of shaking the coins in their pockets and inviting the participants to "show their appreciation in the traditional way" amid much embarrassment for the same participants, many of whom find that it spoils their enjoyment of the tour and, indeed, remains their main memory of it. Professional guiding organisations generally have codes of conduct that prohibit the soliciting of tips and many blue badge guides are too embarrassed by the whole process to attempt it. Everybody has a limit to the things they are prepared to say and do in order to make money and many of us draw the line at asking directly for it in the form of cash.

This might be too coy for some passengers. Many tourists, particularly from the Americas, are only too happy to be told when and how to tip. However, it is important to remember what sort of tour you are conducting. If it is a service tour, where individuals purchase the tour through a brochure and arrive individually or in family groups, then part of the guide or tour director's task is to create a group ethos by spelling out the responsibilities those people have to make the tour successful for all involved. These were set out in chapter two – no smoking on the coach, not holding up everybody else by being late, not talking over the commentary – but sometimes it is a good idea for the guide to suggest some positives and encourage people to ask questions and participate in the tour rather than just sitting and listening. Bouncing ideas off people, finding out where they are from and relating what is said to them makes them feel actively involved in a tour rather just passively listening. In this case, they are far more likely to remember it and to tip well afterwards. A visual reminder might be adequate – a tip basket on a day tour or some envelopes on an extended tour - and at other times a one sentence mention of the subject is permissible. Phrase this sentence in a way which is confident and relaxed and it will pay dividends. Make it too forceful or too ingratiating and it will be both embarrassing and counterproductive.

In contrast to the service tours are private tours. These are groups of people who have travelled together from a particular destination and will return there as a group. They may be from a school, college or retirement community or they might have a common interest in gardens, antiques or sport. They will almost certainly have a group leader of some sort, who might be a professional in tourism or who might simply enjoy putting together a package for his friends and neighbours every year. These group leaders are often priests and some like to start the day with prayers before the guide can start work. In these cases the guide has less work to do in bonding the group but needs to be aware of their particular specialisation or sensitivities.

For private groups it is vital for the guide to establish a working relationship with the tour leader – even if he is a pain in the neck. It is this man (usually) or woman (occasionally) who will guide his charges in the business of tipping and who will provide feedback to the tour operator about the success or otherwise of the tour. Lose him or her and you have lost the group. It may well, in fact, be a couple you have to deal with and then you need some amateur psychology to decide which one is the dominant half of the relationship. And do not assume that, because it is a church group, all will be sweetness and light amongst the brethren. Sometimes it seems that, the more they are committed to spreading peace on earth, the more they like waging war amongst themselves.

With private groups, soliciting tips is almost certainly going to be both distasteful and counterproductive. The group leader will probably have organised something in advance and may even have costed tips into the price of the tour. He will probably also have costed in his own airfare and hotel rooms, if not a profit margin for himself. Habits vary in this area and it is really none of the guide's concern, but it is worth trying to gain the group leader's trust by providing free excursions wherever possible. On a side trip to a cabaret or a boat cruise, most suppliers will not charge for a genuine tour leader and some may take the spouse along free of charge as well. There is, of course, a limit to these freebies, or comps as they are known in the USA, and guides should not try to stretch beyond these limits. The guide will have to return to the same venue later and will need the goodwill, while the tour leader will not.

Sometimes a tour becomes over-burdened with decision makers: a guide, a tour director, a tour leader, a driver, sometimes a representative from the travel agency. This can be very trying for both the ordinary passenger and for the guide, who just wants to build up a rapport with his party yet finds that every decision has to go through a committee of involved parties. Most guides go into the tourist business to get away from that scenario but occasionally it reappears in highly organised group packages which end up being anything but.

In situations like these the guide may find that his or her tip comes in the shape of a discreet envelope from the travel rep who does not want the passengers to be burdened with tipping. This seems a bit pointless as the guide gets his envelope whether he talks non-stop or sleeps through his duties. A tip is supposed to be an individual thank you from the passenger to the guide rather than a guaranteed bonus. Not that any guide ever turns down those discreet envelopes.

On occasions a guide may need to distribute a few discreet envelopes himself, particularly if conducting an extended tour. Many companies cost in a small (sometimes minute) tip for the restaurant staff at hotels or restaurants and advertise the fact in their brochures. This does save the passenger the trouble of dipping into his or her pocket several times a day for small amounts. With our relatively heavy coinage and the need to keep money in a secure place, the attendant frequent removal of clothing all the way down to underwear (and maybe beyond) can be very irritating for the tipper and time-consuming for the tipped, who has to hum and hah, looking anywhere but at the disrobing tourist searching for his or her hidden wallet or purse.

This need to avoid the necessity of passengers having to relentlessly tip is particularly true in third world countries where there is a virtual army of attendants floating around the traveller, all hoping for baksheesh. Conscience and the obvious disparities in wealth between tipper and tipped make the distribution of funds to helpers seem morally obligatory, yet acquiring sufficient small notes and coins can be a real problem and distributing them freely does not buy you extra peace – it merely sets you out as an easy mark. The predetermined tip, while it may seem a contradiction in terms, can make life easier for the tourist on occasions, particularly if he is moving rapidly between currencies and cultures. The guide's job may involve distributing some of these, but he should be very careful not to get sucked into paying too many of these out of his own pocket. The guide is there primarily to earn tips not to pay them.

If he does his job properly, they should come, but they will always be an uncertain source of income, a bonus rather than a basic. Some guides, particularly those who work with groups from non-tipping cultures or who conduct short line of route tours in country houses, might go from one end of a season to the other without seeing a tip. For others, tipping might be the difference between survival and prosperity. All monies earned through tips, of course, are subject to the income tax rates set out in the first paragraph – although you will have to look hard to find a guide who is in the forty per cent tax bracket these days.

CHAPTER SEVEN:

NO LAUGHING MATTER

Humour on tours

Two Americans go into a pub in a British city. It is wet, cold and windy. They order their beers and stand at the bar complaining about the country. One says to the other in exasperation, "This beer is terrible – it is warm and flat. It is always raining here. Those goddam women are so ugly. The food is awful. Jeez, this place must be the arsehole of the world!" The barmaid, listening to this diatribe, leans over and, smiling sweetly, says to them, "Just passing through were you, fellas?"

The joke was originally told about American GIs based in Britain during the war, but it could as well be applied to tourists, like the other and better known crack about them: there are only three things wrong with the yanks – they are overpaid, oversexed and over here. Would a guide tell either of these jokes to his party? The second would probably work – it is actually quite flattering to the outsider to be considered more potent than the insider – but the first is less likely to work. No one is likely to be pleased to be compared to what goes through any backside. It is the sort of joke that might do after a few drinks at the bar but not on the microphone.

There is a fine line between jokes at the expense of people and in conspiracy with them. Many guides make cynical jokes about their passengers which, with a little tweaking, can later be recycled on their tours. Two typical examples concern Windsor Castle. On the way out from London, the eager guide explains to his jet-lagged party all about the history of Windsor from the earliest days, when William the Conqueror built a fortification as part of his beat the Saxons into the ground campaign, to the present when Her Majesty uses it as a summer and weekend residence.

When they reach the coach park and start to walk up to the castle one of the tourists wakes up and, hearing a plane thundering overhead (a common rival at Windsor) asks the guide why the Queen built her castle so close to Heathrow Airport. On the way back the coach goes through Runnymede where the guide explains that King John agreed to the terms of Magna Carta in 1215. Slow-witted Cyrus from Omaha looks at his watch, sees that it is 12:30 and says to his wife, "Darn, we just missed it."

Billy Connolly might not be eating his heart out but both these jokes can work. Like most humour, it needs the spoken voice rather than the written word. The difference between a conspiratorial joke – let us all laugh at the naiveté of tourists together – and the cynical one – aren't you stupid, you are a tourist – can simply depend on the tone of voice of the teller. Most people like to think of themselves as having a self-deprecating sense of humour, being able (and willing) to laugh at themselves. What people do not like is being laughed at.

On one occasion I was talking people through the sights of Edinburgh after we had been out for dinner. Frank from New Zealand was very keen to get to the laundrette on the next day and, for the umpteenth time, reminded me to point it out on the way. "Shut up about the bloody laundrette, Frank" I said over the microphone in a kind of semi-exasperated, affectionate way. Everyone laughed (including Frank) but if I had uttered exactly the same works in a different, harsher tone of voice, with genuine annoyance, the atmosphere would have darkened immediately and I would have had to apologise to Frank and the group to rebuild bridges.

Laughter is one thing which bonds a group of people together, gives them an experience that they can share and remember. It is often one of the most vivid memories of a tour, although it might have nothing to do with the guide, just arising out of someone misunderstanding a local custom or piece of language, a local accent that is hard to understand but easy to make fun of. This kind of humour of circumstance is usually impossible to recreate. In Annie Hall, there is a scene in which Woody Allen's character is shown trying to recreate a farcical lobster cookery session with a new girlfriend that he remembers from his time with Annie. Her response? She lights a cigarette and looks puzzled. Some funny situations are unrepeatable.

Some jokes are also unrepeatable. Sex is one area that should be tiptoed around. For some people on a tour, it is a distant memory. For others it is an item on their agenda. If it is skirted over tactfully, it can provide a good source of humour, particularly if it is tied in with another subject that has cropped up in the course of a tour. Two examples, in the first of which sex is tied with sport, the second with religion:

Two lifelong friends go for their weekly round of golf on Sunday afternoon. They are moaning about how, since the imposition of female equality, they have to share the course with women on Sundays, a day traditionally reserved for the hard-working male. Progress seems particularly slow and they realise that the cause of the delay is two women farther down the course who are taking ages playing their shots. One is about to putt when her friend says to her, "Did I tell you about Mrs Smith?" Gossip, gossip, gossip while play stops. Eventually, the other is about to take her shot, when her companion says, "Wait a minute, I have a new recipe. Write this down." (The teller can play up the male stereotyping – the men come off worse in the end.) Eventually one of the men says to his friend, "I am going to get those women to hurry up or get off the course. We can't have this kind of nonsense." He strides up towards them in high dudgeon, but stops when he gets closer and sees who they are. He then runs back to his old friend who asks him why he chickened out. "Well, I could hardly confront them together when I saw who they were. One is my wife and other is my mistress!" The friend then says, "You are useless. Leave this to me," and he strides along the fairway. Shortly afterwards he too returns to his partner, who asks him why he also failed to confront them. "A small world, isn't it?"

Young Jimmy Murphy goes along to confession. He tells the bored priest about the usual sins – stealing, beating up his brother, cheating in school – but adds a new one. He has become interested in girls and has started experimenting with one of them behind the schoolhouse. The priest's ears prick up and, anxious to make sure that the girl in question later confesses her part in this, tells Jimmy to reveal her name. Jimmy is curiously reluctant until the priest says that he has to know the name of the girl, but Jimmy does not need to say it. He will say a name and, if it is the right one, all Jimmy has to do is tap the side of the confessional box. He goes the names of likely suspects amongst the looser members of his flock – Mary O'Reilly, Sheila O'Casey, Patricia Murphy – until he comes up with the name and Jimmy gives the tap. The priest gives him a severe penance and Jimmy leaves church to be confronted by his friends, who have all making the same experiments, to ask him what happened. Jimmy tells them that there is bad news and good news. What is the bad news, they ask. He runs through the penance they all face. What is the good news, one asks. "Well, I've got the names of another three girls."

Sex plays a part in both of these jokes, but they are not dirty jokes. The first makes fun of both men and golf and works well coming to or from St Andrew's. (It is probably better on the way out - people are more likely to be awake.) The second relies for its effect on the differences between the Protestant and Catholic systems and goes well with a short explanation of the pre-eminence of the Catholic Church in Southern Ireland, in contrast to its historic struggle for survival. Many visitors to Ireland have Catholic backgrounds and enjoy stories that highlight the superiority of their faith over the opposition. A half decent joke is often a good way of rounding out a more serious and detailed explanation.

A similar type of joke can be made about Israel. The country's millionth immigrant came into Tel Aviv airport from the old Soviet Union. His arrival was turned into a media event and reporters went to greet him when he arrived. They started asking him about life in the USSR, but he always gave the same reply. What was your job like? Oh, can't complain. Did you have a nice house? Mmm, can't complain. Did you have a car, good schools, nice holidays? Always the same response – can't complain. Well, why did you come to Israel then, one reporter asked in exasperation: "Because in Israel, you can complain."

And, boy, can they complain. Israelis have a reputation in the business for demanding more than any other nationality and trying to fit more into the day than anyone else. Occasionally they travel in mixed groups but parties of Israelis travelling in a group together are more the norm these days and there are few guides and drivers who fight over those allocations at the expense of, say, groups made up largely of Americans. While some nationalities would not be pleased at being stereotyped as complainers, no Israeli is offended by hearing that joke. They recognise the citizen who is never happy and makes a virtue of complaining, who does not suffer fools gladly. It is a mark of their feistiness, their refusal to lie down in the face of both incompetence and tyranny.

Religion is a good source of jokes, far more so than politics. Political jokes are almost always partisan and only funny to the teller and those whose sympathies he shares. Possibly because people do not take religion as seriously, the subject is usually more fertile. Jokes can be enjoyed by those both inside and outside the faith, particularly if they show that God has a sense of humour. A priest who is a fanatical golf player wakes up on a beautiful Sunday morning desperate for a game. Seeing that it is such a good day, he phones in sick and slips off to the golf course. God and St Peter look down from Heaven and notice him neglecting his parish. St Michael suggests punishing him and God agrees. When the priest takes his first shot it sails down the fairway, lands on the green and he makes a hole in one. "How does that punish him?" asks St Michael. "Who's he going to tell?" replies God.

Jewish jokes are generally off-limits because they tip over into negative stereotyping and this then turns into racism, which has no place in tourism. This is not being sanctimonious. Tourism relies on people travelling from one culture to another and experiencing the differences between them. There is a degree of respect in this process. The whole exercise is pointless if people are prejudged in a dismissive way, so the confirmed racist is simply wasting his time travelling to see the culture of another country. Stereotyping only works in guides' jokes if there is an element of flattery in it – the apparently simple Irish catholic boy who finds out who the loose girls are from his priest (you never get leads like that in a Protestant chapel) or the Russian Jew who looks forward to living in Israel so he can be as cantankerous as the next citizen.

The guide can always make a few jokes against his own nationality. Or nationalities in the case of Britain, a country where four distinct national groups each exist under the same government. A ship is wrecked in the ocean and eight survivors swim to a deserted island. Two are English, two Welsh, two Scots and two Irish. Stranded for years they form a society that reflects their national characteristics. The two Welshmen form a choir, the two Scots open a bank and the two Irish start up a pub (or a civil war). But the two Englishmen? They stay on opposite sides of the island without speaking. Why? Because they have not been introduced, of course. This kind of joke works well enough in context, as a rider to an explanation of how the British peoples have a primary loyalty to their own small country but they are also citizens of the United Kingdom. It is the English who are usually the butt of these jokes, making up for centuries of dismissive stereotyping of their neighbours.

If the joke is against the teller's own group or nationality it is hard to be offended by it. At The Changing of the Guard, people are impressed that the soldiers march down the Mall with such perfect discipline as they approach Buckingham Palace. This, however, is not just a tourist spectacle and it is worth the guide pointing out that these men are serving soldiers in the British army. There are subtle differences in the uniforms of the different Guards regiments which can identify whether they are Coldstream, Grenadier, Welsh, Irish or Scots Guards, all with their own tradition and military history. It was the discipline of these soldiers that defeated all our enemies in Europe, particularly the French armies of Louis XIV and Napoleon. Then we fought against the Americans. Now, this nationality has never fully understood the art of warfare properly – they used to hide behind trees and take pot shots at our chaps whose red jackets made perfect targets. The rugged American sharpshooter made good against the hidebound British army. This sort of bloodthirsty humour goes down very well if told with a self-deprecating shrug, although the soldiers on the receiving end were probably not that amused.

If an American party responds to this kind of humour, they might enjoy the story of London Bridge. This is a tale often miss-told by complacent Britons making fun of foolish Americans. The myth is that the man who bought London Bridge in the early seventies thought that he was really buying Tower Bridge, which is far more visually spectacular but which is un-sellable, so much have its towers become part of the London skyline. In fact, the American businessman Robert McCulloch knew exactly what he was doing when he bought the bridge which was no longer strong enough to take the weight of heavy traffic passing over it every day, and which needed rebuilding. In 1970 he paid the City of London Corporation a million pounds, shipped the bridge to Lake Havasu in Arizona and sat back to count his money. Property sales at his Havasu retirement community jumped from one a half million dollars a month to a million dollars a week after the bridge arrived and there is now a permanent population there of over 50,000 who can see a bit of Olde England without having to get onto an aeroplane.

There may be a sucker born every minute but it was not the man who bought London Bridge. He laughed all the way to the bank.

A guide can have a bit of fun with this story. It is not so much a joke with a punch line but an amusing anecdote which can be told to show the outsider having the last laugh. What do you with an old bridge that is no use to anyone? Obvious really, you ship it five thousand miles away and stick it in the middle of a desert. But the chap who did it knew exactly what he was about, and the next time we sell you a bridge we are going to ask a lot more for than a million for it. This is one of those stories on the margin. It can easily slip from self-deprecation (of the British who sold their bridge far too cheaply) to sneering (at the stupid Americans who bought the useless thing). No country is more sensitive to feelings of persecution and the mockery than the USA. This is particularly true after September 11th 2001, when they had to watch not only images of their country being attacked but of people in the Arab world celebrating the fact. A soft touch is in order with jokes about Americans.

Australians, on the other hand, actually prefer something more heavy-handed. They love to be teased and taunted in the rare case of an English victory over them in the field of sport, when they have a 'give as good as you get' attitude. They expect a bit of gloating and will return it with interest when they have the opportunity. They particularly like jokes about cricket, an incomprehensible activity to most Americans who have no idea what the phrase "Ray Illingworth is just relieving himself at the Nursery End" means. Test Match Special on the radio was famous for these double entendres, most of which were deliberate, some of which were accidental. John Arlott certainly was well-prepared when the West Indian bowler Michael Holding was coming up to bowl to the English batsman Peter Willey and came out with, "The bowler's Holding, the batsman's Willey".

Everybody can enjoy the rules of cricket with all its ins and outs. There are two teams in a cricket match. Each team has eleven players. When one side is in, each man that is in the team that is in goes out, and then he stays in until he is out, when he comes back in again. And then the next man is in and he goes out. When each man that is in the team that is in has been out, the team that has been out comes in and the team that has been in goes out and tries to get those who are coming in out. When each man on both sides has been in and out twice, including the not outs, that is the end of the game.

Every Australian, cricket fan or not, will recognise the linguistic absurdities of this factually correct description, just as they will recognise the Willey, Holding and Illingworth sentences. For them cricket humour is the humour of familiarity. For Americans and other non-Commonwealth countries, it is the humour of the absurd, recognisable only in quaint phrases such as 'it's just not cricket' or 'he's on a sticky wicket there'. Australians like jokes about cricket, not only because they are good at it, but because it provides them with a frame of reference in a foreign country, where they might otherwise feel neglected and ignored. People can easily become chippy and defensive if they feel that their own achievements are being ignored when they come to see the treasures of other countries, so a reference back to their native talents or character can be very reassuring. Otherwise they are more likely to continually bring the conversation back to their own country and how important it is in the scheme of things.

Sometimes people chip in with jokes of their own. Many of these are pretty feeble or too local to be appreciated by another nationality. Occasionally one works. A lady on a tour suddenly feels the need to go to the toilet. At the time I had been telling the group about the Free Presbyterian Church in Scotland. Known affectionately as the 'wee frees', their members have strong views on the sanctity of the Sabbath and the wickedness of almost all other sects. Eric Liddell, the runner known as the flying Scot, was one of their number and his refusal to break the ban on Sunday sport was part of the subject of the film Chariots of Fire.

Interrupting my story, I find the nearest loo, but the lady concerned is annoyed to find that she has to pay twenty pence to use it. She remarks as she returns, "Eddie, you can keep the wee frees - just find me a free wee next time." That crack has been recycled many times to good effect.

Another one comes from the Changing of the Guard ceremony. The crowds are controlled by mounted police who need to keep traffic, soldiers and spectators separate. On a particularly busy and hot day the jostling of the crowds is not helped by an animal lover who castigates a female police officer for not taking care of her mount properly. Look at that animal, it is so hot and sweaty, he calls out to her. You'd be pretty hot and sweaty, sir, if you had been between my legs for the last two hours, she replies without breaking stride. The horse lover is silenced and the crowd shows marked respect for the frank policewoman.

Where do jokes come from in the first place? A science fiction story of many years ago had a team of aliens living in a hideaway manufacturing jokes which they surreptitiously introduce into the human community, and it sometimes seems that some jokes just appear from nowhere. Most, however, probably originate from professional gag writers who supply stand-up comedians with their own stock of jokes that can be honed into shape onstage. Tour groups often make up the bulk of the audience for cabarets featuring these comedians, but the guides and tour directors are unlikely to be seen in the audience. They know that they can virtually set their watches by the timing of the jokes as they come in a predictable and well-organised sequence. These shows are particularly popular in Ireland, a country which has long traded on its reputation for whimsical humour.

Comedians make a little extra by selling and signing tapes and compact discs of their act and sometimes they provide a welcome diversion on a long and not especially interesting stretch of road. (Almost all coaches have cassette players and some play CDs as well.) The Irish comedian Hal Roach has helped many a tour through a traffic jam when people are starting to get bored, and Bob Newhart's famous sketch The Introduction of Tobacco to Civilisation is a good way of adding a lighter touch to the achievements and character of Walter Raleigh. As with the comedians on stage, however, the group may be laughing at the jokes on the tape but the driver and guide are more likely to be looking stony-faced at the road or reading the newspaper. The humour only lasts so long and wears off a few outings. In fact, to look at guides and drivers when a comedy tape is playing on the coach, you might think that telling jokes can be a grim business. As Oscar Wilde said of the German sense of humour – it is no laughing matter.

CHAPTER EIGHT:
STONE CIRCLES AND WHITE HORSES
Guiding and archaeology

Agatha Christie, who was married to one, said that an archaeologist was the best husband a woman could wish for because he grew more interested in her the older she became. It was a clever comment from a woman who had endured her share of marital trauma and was glad to settle down with someone who had the self-confidence to be unbothered by her murderous success. She probably also enjoyed the clue-hunting aspect of archaeology.

In her day it was the preserve of men like Alexander Keiller, whose fortune came from the family marmalade firm, and Gilbert Insall, the First World War pilot who discovered Woodhenge from the air. It was an upper-class hobby for people who were too serious to spend their money on hunting or gambling but too grand to work. One of the first men to become a professional archaeologist was Geoffrey Wainwright, a Welsh miner's son, despite (or because) he was warned that he would need a private income to pursue his passion.

Through the efforts of men like Wainwright and the discoveries unearthed by the early amateurs, archaeology has become a respectable academic profession. However, there are still plenty of worker-ants needed in digs, which tend to be uncomfortable, back-bending affairs. They are supervised by a few professionals and staffed by an army of volunteers, working for expenses, refreshments and glory if they are lucky. It may be great fun but it is not much of a way to earn a living.

Some people trained in archaeology end up as tourist guides and many guides have a background in the subject. Some knowledge of it is essential if you are to provide a reasonably accurate picture of the past. Written records are pretty skimpy before Bede, who lived in seventh century Newcastle, and non-existent before the Romans. The tendency is to assume that, if we do not have any writings from the period, we can dismiss the people, but one thing a guide can point out is that there is a difference between primitive and prehistoric. Primitive might mean savage, but prehistoric is simply from before written records existed (or were preserved).

Most people have a sense of this when they go to Stonehenge. It is one of those key sites people around the world have heard of. They may get confused between different churches and castles, kings and knights, but they know about and have seen images of this ancient monument in Wiltshire a few miles north of Salisbury. In fact, it is often cited as "the reason we came on this tour" and it is included in most itineraries as a stop of about forty five minutes to an hour. That may not seem like a long time for Britain's most famous temple, but it is often exposed to a biting wind, which discourages lingering, and the time coincides with what a coach driver needs for a compulsory break. It is long enough for people to visit the toilets and shop or listen to the automated tour on the handsets supplied by English Heritage, who maintain the site.

Or what is left of it. Many people will have a memory of Stonehenge when you were able to walk amongst the stones. (I have a childhood memory of sitting on the so-called Slaughter Stone once on a family picnic.) This ceased to be possible in 1977 when the stones were fenced in. With around three quarters of a million visitors a year, it soon became obvious that unsupervised access would damage the monument further than it had been already, so in the late seventies it was roped off and people were no longer able to touch the stones.

Almost ever since, there has been a debate about what to do next. Periodically, Stonehenge is described as "a national disgrace" and the need to revamp the site is promoted. Plans are underway to take the nearby A303 through a tunnel and possibly build a new interpretation centre where the roundabout now is. This will necessitate a long walk for tourists, not usually noted for their ambulatory enthusiasm, and will be accompanied by the right to walk amongst the stones – but not to touch them. How one will be allowed but not the other remains to be explained. When, if, these plans do come to fruition an hour will no longer be enough.

Stonehenge has, in fact, been altered in relatively recent times. Although only around two thirds of the original stones are still there, many of these were re-erected and probably moved slightly from their original position in a fit of Edwardian improvement in the early twentieth century. The concrete used to support one of the large stones can be quite clearly seen as you walk around the path. It is interesting to contrast the Stonehenge of today with the pre-improved version in the paintings of Constable and Turner.

What is now proposed by English Heritage and the various interested parties goes far beyond this Edwardian exercise in tidying up and clarification. Although they will adjust to whatever finally materialises there, many guides are unenthusiastic about these improvement schemes. (My heart sinks when I hear the phrase interpretation centre.) Partly this is the egotism of the guide. Hey, that is our job, we say. It is also because we are afraid that Stonehenge will lose some of its magic, rather than gain it, through over-interpretation. At the moment it is like a blank piece of paper which people can write on themselves. The danger is that it will become a form that has been filled in.

The concept of minimalism has never been very strong in tourism. People respond more to magnificence – soaring arches, bright colours and over the top opulence. And no-one can claim that the facilities at Stonehenge are world class – an entrance booth, a coffee stall (the rock cakes are good, really) and a shop, all hidden from view. But this is surely the point. When you stand by the heel stone you can see the horizon on a clear sweep at a roughly equal distance for 360 degrees around you, just as your ancestors could. The minimal, or minimalist, facilities are out of sight, tactfully built below the level of the ground at the entrance, and access to the stones comes along a tunnel. The present coach and car park is even close enough to the stones for some companies to skimp on the entrance fee and leave people to walk across the busy road to look at them from the wrong side of the fence. English Heritage is trying to discourage this kind of suicide tourism by levying a high parking fee on coaches whose passengers do not have the entrance fee included in their tour.

This leads us inevitably to the three 'v's of tour company brochures. Both tourists and guides need to learn about the subtleties of phrasing in apparently seductive brochures. If a brochure says "we drive via Stonehenge", it means that you are not guaranteed a stop there and can only hope that the guide gives his passengers some time for one or that the driver at least changes to a lower gear as you drive by. If it then says "we view Salisbury Cathedral", that means exactly what it says – you get to see it but not necessarily to go inside. If you do have time to go in, you will probably have to pay your own entrance fee/donation (see the chapter on Church Going). Only if the wording of the itinerary says that "we visit the Roman Baths" can you be sure that an entrance fee is costed in to the price of the tour. A "via" can mean simply a drive past; "view" commits a company to nothing more than a brief photograph stop within a reasonable distance of the site; but a "visit" commits the operator to the cost of the ticket inside. The above three items, by the way, are perfectly viable on a day trip from London, although it would be Stonehenge that attracts people onto the trip, so it should be prioritised by the guide, if not by the operator.

Guides learn to get a feel for the appetite of their charges for each one of these 'v's. It is easy to overestimate their capacity for visits and slip into ABC syndrome (see

Church Going again). On the other hand, nothing is more frustrating than constantly photographing the outside of interesting looking places without having time to go inside. Explaining that this or that visit is not included in the tour is sometimes necessary, but it might be worth adding that they will be going inside the castle in, for example, Edinburgh or Windsor where a visit is usually included. If there are a lot of views and vias on a tour, a guide can gain some points by organising a visit or two, if time permits.

A via would never be adequate for Stonehenge, although a view might have to suffice. If a visit has not been costed in, this is one of those places where the guide might organise it for his passengers. Most sites offer discounts for groups and senior citizens, and it is sensible to round out the cost so that each passenger can give, say, five pounds to the guide for their entrance and then have the satisfaction of going straight through the entrance gate while everyone else fumbles for change or credit cards. One of the advantages of group touring over individual travel is that you are able to jump queues at popular sites, and the satisfaction of doing so generally outweighs the irritation of the extra expense. And would a guide ever make a profit for himself in the process by taking advantage of the discounts for groups/senior citizens? Perish the thought.

What will you find out in an hour's visit? You will see something of the world of our ancestors, what the archaeologist Mike Pitts calls Hengeworld. You will have an idea of when Stonehenge was built, between four and five thousand years ago, where the stones came from and who erected them. You should know that the sun rises above the Heel Stone on midsummer morning when viewed from the centre of the circle and sets in the opposite direction on midwinter eve. You may gather that there are two types of stones – the large Sarsen stones from the nearby Marlborough Downs and the smaller bluestones from South Wales – and that the bumps in the ground around them on the Salisbury Plain are the graves of people who were

114

involved in the construction and use of the site.

You will probably also find that there are a large number of legends surrounding Stonehenge. Each generation reinvents it in a different way. It has been a burial place for King Arthur, a place of worship and sacrifice for Druids, even a proof of interplanetary travel by aliens who provided the foundations of our civilisation in the writings of Erich von Daneken. It has been painted and photographed innumerable times, featured in films and stories, and an internet search on Stonehenge reveals around 200,000 sites.

For years it attracted a pilgrimage of new age hippies around midsummer until the damage done to the area became intolerable and they were banned. Giving high-spending overseas tourists priority over freeloading native dropouts caused a good deal of resentment at the time and a police presence was necessary at the monument for several years to prevent the diehards of the midsummer festival returning. It is sad in a way that modern tourism was incompatible with the alternative lifestyle of the festival, but the community that took part in it was simply too undisciplined to guarantee that the site and the surroundings would not be damaged. They now celebrate midsummer at Glastonbury, that other centre of alternative mystical excess.

Stonehenge also has its own literature. Poems and novels have been based around it, and it slips into books in some memorable scenes. Hardy's Tess of the d'Urbevilles is finally captured there when the President of the Immortals has finished his sport with her, while Robert Graves' Claudius describes the human sacrifices committed by the native British at a thinly disguised but unnamed Stonehenge. In John Fowles' early novel The Magus the narrator has a memorable night time visit there in the time before the fences were put up. Fowles is obviously fascinated by the place and has written a book, The Enigma of Stonehenge, in which he vents his spleen at tourism, fake mysticism, scientific analysis and all the other aspects of modern life that he feels remove the magic from Stonehenge.

Although I am part of that modern apparatus, I have far more sympathy with Fowles than with those who make nonsensical claims for the place. Erich von Daniken is still selling books that promote the idea of alien visitations that gave us civilisation in a pre-packaged form and then left. Whatever his crimes against the intellect, von Daniken was shockingly treated by the Swiss authorities who imprisoned him, ostensibly for a few minor financial indiscretions, in reality for contradicting the popular perception of the Swiss as a reliable and unimaginative race. He has since taken up residence in California where his overactive imagination is a positive qualification for adoption by the locals.

Another seventies writer, the late Gerald Hawkins, wrote a well researched and imaginative book, Stonehenge Decoded, in which he put forward the idea that the people who built Stonehenge could anticipate eclipses by tracing the paths of not only the sun but also the moon and could then predict when their paths would coincide. Daringly, Hawkins used a computer to analyse the data that led to these conclusions, but sadly his ideas, which inspired many people to visit and study Stonehenge, are now largely discredited.

Mike Pitts says on his website that the majority of the claims made for the scientific and astronomical abilities of the henge builders are "patronising nonsense". It is just as easy - and as misguided - to overestimate as to underestimate the abilities of our ancestors. Turning them into some kind of scientific super sleuths does rather beg the question of why they lived such short and uncomfortable lives. The normal life span of the people buried in the Salisbury Plain barrows is around twenty five to thirty years and they surely believed in an afterlife because they are buried with pottery beakers presumably used to take food and drink into the next world. In fact, they are often referred to as Beaker People, although this term is no longer fashionable in archaeological circles.

It is a useful non-technical phrase though, more so than Neolithic, which sounds academic and alienating. People can identify with their Beaker predecessors and I use it as a shorthand term. Shorthand is a good analogy for guiding. It needs to be both quick and accurate, a clear way of conveying ideas and facts. "Too much information", the fashionable put-down for verbosity, is something guides are often prone to. Guiding examinations are about not drying up, keeping a flow of continuous and interesting commentary, always having something to say, but real tourism is about conveying clear and concise concepts in a more limited time. The attention spans of most people start to wander after around ten minutes of listening so guides need to develop ways of being pithy and precise in bringing over their main points, particularly on a vehicle moving at fifty to sixty miles per hour on a warm day.

One of the points worth bringing across about Stonehenge is that it is not an isolated occurrence but merely the most sophisticated of the many stone circles to be found in the British Isles. Twenty miles to the north stands Silbury Hill, Europe's largest manmade hill, and the massive Avebury stone circle. If Stonehenge seems like old hat or is too commercialised and overcrowded, try going to Avebury. The stones there date from around the same time as those at Stonehenge but are not cut as smoothly or arranged in the tight circle or horseshoe shapes found at its more famous neighbour. Nowhere at Avebury did the builders raise thirty ton blocks of sandstone ten feet above ground and then place them gingerly along the horizontal across two standing stones, as they did at Stonehenge. Yet the sheer scale of the Avebury circle is enormously impressive. They circle part of the village and you can walk right up to them and touch them if you like. At the museum named after Alexander Keiller you can also see his car, an enormous vintage machine that he could convert into sleeping quarters when out looking at prehistoric sites.

Other stone circles can be found around the British Isles for those who are prepared to take a detour to find them. A short turn off the main Oxford-Stratford road leads to the Rollright Stones, frozen knights and kings of old according to legend. There is one in the Lake District, the Castlerigg Circle near Keswick, where the Bee Gees posed for one of their album covers. It is a squeeze but you can take a coach up the farm road that leads there and there is a wonderful view on a fine day towards Skiddaw to the north and Helvellyn to the south. Two can be seen in the Scottish highlands, the Clava Cairns near the Culloden battlefield site and a curious one next to Aviemore Fire Station and there is a beautiful chambered tomb called Maes Howes, built around the time of Stonehenge, on Orkney, which also has an alignment with the midsummer sunrise. Isolated rural places are where to see stone circles: unnumbered ones are buried under motorways and high rise blocks.

There are several in Wales but most of these are modern. When the Welsh get together to sing and celebrate their nationhood in the annual eisteddfod, they leave a stone circle to mark the site. The venue switches from north to south Wales each year and is very much a national (and nationalistic) event. It should not be confused with the international eisteddfod that takes place in Llangollen every year, when people from around the world are invited to sing and compete with each other. For good measure they have a stone circle at Llangollen, but this too is modern.

It is easy to lump together all undated monuments as the work of an ancient and mysterious race, when closer inspection reveals that many of them are relatively recent. This particularly applies to hillside carvings such as white horses. The standing white horse was a symbol of the Hanoverian royal house and it became a fashion in the eighteenth century to advertise your loyalty to the crown by having a horse carved on the hillside near to your home. If the rock underneath is chalk, as it is in much of southern England, the whiteness of the exposed stone contrasts with the greenness around it and, on a clear day, can be seen for miles around. The white horse near Westbury, Somerset is the most obvious one for a guide to point out. Just after the

Somerset sign on the Salisbury to Bath road is the time to turn your head to the right (if travelling to Bath) and, on a clear day, you can see the horse about five miles away. It was fashioned by a Mr Gee in 1778 and is definitely not prehistoric. There is a similar eighteenth century white horse at Kilburn just north of York seen clearly from the A19 on the road to Thirsk. Although these rather solid horses are Georgian in both origin and character, they sometimes stand on the site of older carvings that are not visible to the eye except at close quarters. As with cathedrals, people often want one date when a sequence would be more accurate.

There are older carvings on the hillsides of England, but very few of them can be dated with any degree of certainty. The beautiful white horse of Uffington is the best known example and inspired G K Chesterton's poem:

Before the gods that made the gods
Had seen the sunrise pass
The White Horse of the White Horse Vale
Was cut out of the grass.

This is a far more dynamic beast than the later ones, but none of these horses, static or prancing, will ever get more than a via, a view at most. They need constant maintenance and this is traditionally provided by locals who selflessly keep their outlines fresh and clearly visible, although English Heritage now takes some responsibility for the horses at Uffington and Westbury.

Even the well-known human figures on the hillside are of doubtful antiquity. The Long Man of Wilmington in Sussex is the world's largest representation of a human being. It is probably pre-medieval but has been altered considerably over the centuries and is now not even a chalk outline but stone blocks laid out in lines. It is also demurely un phallic and probably more suitable for a respectable photograph stop than its more famous cousin, the Cerne Abbas giant. There he stands in Dorset five miles north of

Dorchester with his famous upstanding penis waving his club at us, inviting us to be shocked at such aggressive and unapologetic sexuality. He was thought to date from the second century AD when the Roman emperor Commodus set himself up as a reincarnation of Hercules. (I had not heard of him either – generally, the less their achievements, the greater their self-esteem.) It might even have earlier Celtic origins, but no documentary evidence of it exists before 1730. Could it be an ancient pagan fertility symbol or a piece of eighteenth century bawdiness in the character of Rowlandson and Hogarth? Could it have survived the disapproval of the nearby monastery and the Cromwellian killjoys or was local protectiveness towards it so strong that it remained untouched and proudly erect for centuries? At present no-one is sure.

Archaeology can answer some of these questions about the creations of our ancestors, but by no means all. It shines a light on certain parts of the ancient world but never fully illuminates it. Occasionally, it will debunk a fanciful idea, sometimes confirm an old belief. The eighteenth century antiquary William Stukeley looked at the stones of Avebury and became sure that they stretched along a certain path, the Beckhampton Avenue. This frequently derided idea was shown to be largely correct when archaeologists from Southampton University uncovered a large Sarsen stone pretty much exactly where Stukeley expected it to be.

At the same time, the sheer number and inconsistent quality of ancient sites discovered and examined surely gives the lie to the belief that civilisation was imposed on us from above by an alien race. These are the work of peoples struggling to get beyond mere survival, attempting to communicate with their gods and to leave something for future generations while at the same time honouring their ancestors. They erect stone circles at important meeting places, bury their dead in great tombs and maybe celebrate military victory or sexual prowess through carvings on their hillsides (although we should be careful not to put the dinosaur in the same frame as the stone age beauty with her fur bikini portrayed by Raquel Welch in One Million Years BC).

Archaeologists are the scientists of history, examining the physical evidence left to us by our ancestors, while guides are the interpreters of this evidence. One profession is concerned with the minute details, the other with the broad outlines of the past. The archaeologist is the detective looking for clues, the guide is the judge summing up the case (with the tourists as the jury). Modern archaeologists like Mike Pitts have developed sophisticated techniques, undreamt of in the days of Agatha Christie, with which they can examine the past. Although they cannot (yet) date the erection of stones directly, they can use radio carbon dating techniques on the antler tools that the builders discarded after the stones were put up. From this it is a short step to decide when the various parts of Stonehenge were built. They have come up with the date 2350 BC when it is believed that much of the monument as we know it was erected.

This sounds suspiciously precise, but Mike has confidence in the date. In his book Hengeworld (highly recommended but not for those looking for easy answers) he explains some of the methods of modern archaeology, comparing it with the methods of past masters. One of the striking things is how, as well as becoming more precise, archaeology has become more co-operative. In the past it was the maverick individual with a passion for the past who charged into a site and began digging relentlessly until he found what he was looking for. Typical of these men was Hienrich Schliemann, the unearther of Troy, whose methods would have him banned from all digs in the modern world. Now it is university departments and publicly funded bodies who establish large, hierarchical teams where it seems that every grain of dirt has to be catalogued and analysed. The new archaeology is far more thorough, but much less romantic.

While Hengeworld is complex and only partially understood, guides need to deal in the definite and try to keep things clear and simple. Inevitably they sometimes slip across the border from clarification to over-simplification in their desire to engage their passengers. Never let the truth get in a way of a good story, runs the cynical journalists' maxim and maybe guides have more in common with journalists, the ultimate simplifiers, than with archaeologists, the technicians, who revel in the complexities of the world.

At what stage is this unjustified? When does the guide go beyond what is permissible in the interests of clarity? The short answer is that he has carte blanche as far as his tour is concerned. Guiding is one of the last absolute dictatorships, where guides are unrestrained by the demands of supervisors and assessors. Perhaps that is why the romantic and reckless pioneers of archaeology have so much appeal to us. Like all dictators they need to have their fingers on the pulse of their supporters. If they alienate their audience they are lost, if they keep them they can stay in power.

What about a wider duty to the truth? I quoted the journalists' maxim about truth and a good story to a guide at Caernarvon Castle once. His more precise explanation rather undermined my story about how Edward I made his son Prince of Wales so that the Welsh could have a prince born in their country to look after their interests. We laughed about it at the time and agreed that he would concentrate on accuracy and I would deal with truth, which we could regard as a more fluid concept. We were both right in our own ways. I wanted to explain to a sleepy group who had just come off the Irish ferry how the king wanted to unite (or maybe subject) the countries of the British Isles through his rule. He had the sense and tact to see that the Welsh needed a leader they could identify with so he chose his own son for the role. The precise details of the story are malleable and not fully known but the gist is true and Wales has been closer to England ever since, in contrast to Scotland, where

Edward's methods of assimilation were altogether less delicate – and less effective. The group, who overheard the exchange, were unfazed by the discussion. They knew that I was dealing with the broad brush, he with the finer details, although there may be times when the two are simply not compatible.

I suppose the answer is that, if you respect the past, you are allowed to simplify it. If, in this process of simplification, you denigrate it, then you have failed. No-one knows exactly what happened fifty or five hundred, let alone five thousand, years ago. Even when the facts seem certain debate usually follows. The most distinguished historians lock themselves into dispute over the relevance and interpretation of facts that they agree on. The tourist guide can only hope to give a flavour of what life was like in the past, not a comprehensive picture.

A football manager once said that the players only remember the last two things you say to them before they go out on the pitch, so you should keep it simple. If the same is true of tourists (and two may be optimistic in some cases) then I would say the messages of Stonehenge are, "Do not underestimate your ancestors – and let your imagination work here." While I have the greatest respect for the new and increasingly accurate archaeology, I do not think it will help the imagination to work. Let us hope that lack of money and the bureaucratic wrangling of the British planning system combine to keep the old Stonehenge for at least a while longer.

THE SHAKESPEARE MYTH

Why the authorship question is important

It is probably not a good idea to be too messianic as a tour guide. People do not go on holiday to be converted to a cause. They are more likely to want to escape the constraints of morality and responsibility that surround their everyday lives. This can lead to some pretty uninhibited behaviour. Some men travel abroad specifically to experience sex in a way that would not be possible at home. Women are not normally so blatant but can be quite adventurous if the opportunity arises and behave with the kind of abandon they would not dream of showing in their domestic lives. Both sexes usually revert to conventional habits once they return home.

Despite the occasional loss of inhibitions, most passengers on a coach tour tend to be conservative in nature – both politically and socially. They are typically hard-working sensible people with a stake in society, stable marriages, savings and property. They usually have children and often grandchildren and need to bring presents back for those at home. They will not give up their respectability easily and are unlikely to challenge conventional wisdom very strongly. They are, in short, bourgeois.

The guide should never overestimate the knowledge of his passengers – but equally he should not underestimate their intelligence. Most people will have heard of Christopher Wren but it is stupid, even insulting, to refer to "Wren's great classically styled cathedral of St Paul's". It makes those who have not heard of Wren and do not understand classical, as opposed to gothic, feel ignorant and defensive. Even those who are aware of who he is can feel disoriented by the assumptions implicit in mentioning his name without expansion. Wren had an interesting life and it is worth introducing some of it when visiting St Paul's.

It is dangerous for a guide to talk down to a tourist, yet it is surprisingly easy to do so. People hate being preached to or told what to think when on holiday. There is a passage in Barchester Towers by Anthony Trollope in which he bemoans the captivity endured by the church-goer when listening to a sermon. There is no escape: social inhibitions are such that no-one walks out of a church because they are bored by the preacher, so they endure it. The modern equivalent of this is the guided tour – people have invested too much to leave. Where would they go? Their hotel rooms are booked, they have a seat on the coach and they want to see the places they are going to, so they will sit through almost any amount of boredom to get there.

Nevertheless, a few enthusiasms are no bad thing for a guide. If what you care about is non-political it will be a lot easier to introduce it into your tour. Shakespeare is one of my enthusiasms and he comes into most tours at some time. There used to be little opportunity to mention him on a London tour – a statue in Poet's Corner at Westminster Abbey and one in the British Museum, plus an obscure plaque in Southwark that would only be seen on a walking tour or a visit to the nearby Anchor Pub. However, once the American actor Sam Wannamaker set about recreating the Globe Theatre Shakespeare became more visibly a part of the London landscape, a useful photo stop near the Tate Modern across the Thames from St Paul's. You can even walk there over the new footbridge now that they have fixed it.

Wannamaker's dream was a particularly American one, a kind of extension of the tourist industry. No native Londoner would have dared suggest rebuilding Shakespeare's theatre on the south bank of the Thames. What we produced instead is the South Bank about a mile away, the concrete complex that includes the National Theatre, Festival Hall and Hayward Gallery. The National attracts some of the world's best actors and directors, while the Globe was the brainchild of an under extended

Hollywood actor, conceived as a grand personal campaign during his life but only completed after his death. Yet the Globe is a far more welcoming building which people appreciate taking time to look at and visit for its own sake.

It took an outsider to do this, someone used to concrete but still thrilled by thatch and wood. For many British people it smacked of historical re-enactment societies, bank managers pretending to be roundheads or cavaliers at the weekend, alright for a bit of fun or as backdrop to a film, but somehow not serious. It was a Euro Disney scheme, ye Olde Shakespeare project for those who had heard of him but who had never sat through one of his plays. Wannamaker appeared in some pretty average films and television to pay for his dream. The Globe was his serious moment, a dream that we could see Shakespeare's plays as he would have when he was alive in the city where he wrote most of them.

There is no need to mock what Wannamaker achieved. The plays are well performed and received. There are no hidden microphones or jarring effects. It is about as close to Elizabethan Shakespeare as most of us will get and there is something both moving and triumphant about the way the plays are produced in this setting. Why is this? Probably because of the attention paid to the materials used. Concrete was necessary for the National, a building designed to be impressive rather than warm. It is the builder's plastic, practical but unwelcoming. And it does not mellow with age. There are signs of wear and decay as the National's concrete has been assaulted by London's weather and pollution but it does not make the building seem any more loveable.

When the new Globe was built, however, they took enormous care to use the right materials, scouring the country for oak beams that were tall enough to support the walls, using the same materials and methods as the original builders. This has not been a complete success and there is a certain irony in the fact that, as I write, builders are digging up the lime and hazelnut floor to replace it with a concrete one for the new season. Modern footwear and posture proved to be incompatible with Elizabethan flooring. Safety regulations also meant that the new theatre had to have four doors instead of the original two and a sprinkler system for the thatched roof. This roof is made from Norfolk reed and gained the first permit for the use of thatch in central London since the great fire of 1666. Allowing for modern fire regulations and audience comfort, the building has a surprising integrity and, along with the London Eye, has brought quite a few tour groups to the south side of the Thames, where they rarely ventured before. It is the opposite of the effects used in theme parks, where plastic imitates stone or wood.

But what about the integrity of Shakespeare's identity? While it is easy to idolise Shakespeare beyond his abilities and ignore his mistakes, it is also easy to trivialise him by questioning whether he actually wrote the plays and poems attributed to him. Did Shakespeare, from a small town in the middle of England, with no advantages of birth or education, really write all those great works, people wonder. Surely it was someone else, with more education and a grander background who must have done it for him and used his name. Even the museum at the Globe gives an airing to this idea.

This question of Shakespeare's identity keeps cropping up like an un killable monster, a successful Hollywood franchise. No matter that there is a wealth of evidence to tie William Shakespeare of Stratford to the works in his name, or that there could be no good reason for a genius of Shakespeare's magnitude to hide his talent, the question sooner or later is asked on Stratford or London tours. Did he really write the plays? Wasn't it Bacon, Oxford, Marlowe? The BBC has devoted at least two programmes to the authorship question, articles appear in travel magazines and books are written on it. The belief that Shakespeare was a substitute has a life of its own. And plenty of tourist guides exploit it to keep a tour alive. Yet it is a completely bogus idea. No serious scholar believes it, so why should anyone else? It is worth examining this phenomenon and see why

Shakespeare's works could not possibly have been written by someone else.

The irony is, of course, that Shakespeare had a classic writer's background - middle-class gentility fallen on hard times. Graham Greene once said that there was a shaft of ice in the heart of every writer and one can often see how it develops by looking at their childhoods. Read Sons and Lovers (D H Lawrence), A House for Mr Biswas (V S Naipaul) or The Mill on the Floss (George Eliot). All are heavily autobiographical novels: in them you can see how the writer as a child observes the way a much-loved parent comes to terms with disappointment and disgrace and resolves to do better himself. There is something of this in Jane Austen as well, the dreaded fall from respectability, the struggle to keep up appearances, the restoration of the family fortune, through hard work, good luck or romantic rescue. The same process is seen in the only other writer to rival Shakespeare in combining popular success and the respect of posterity.

The similarities between the lives of William Shakespeare and Charles Dickens are not often commented on, yet they had curiously similar lives and backgrounds. Both men were the sons of failed businessmen, bankrupts who were never able to pay the bills. As each entered the susceptible age of puberty things got particularly bad. Dickens' traumas at this time are well known and he used them to great effect later, particularly in David Copperfield and Little Dorrit - the blacking factory, his father John's imprisonment, family disgrace and tension. We know less about Shakespeare's father, also John, but records tell us that at one stage he was unable to leave the family home, so afraid was he of being arrested for debt and that he could not pay the interest on the money he owed.

Did Shakespeare's father inspire Falstaff in the way that Dickens' is believed to have inspired Micawber? This idea has the ring of truth about it – Falstaff has the same first name and there is a good deal in Henry IV about fathers and sons, just as there is a good deal in late Shakespeare about fathers and daughters. Of course, much of this is speculation with about as much justification as that of those who credit Bacon or Marlowe. The parallels between the two men do not stop there, however.

After the traumas of family disgrace when growing up came a kind of independence through early marriage. Shakespeare was eighteen when he married Anne Hathaway, eight years his senior, while Dickens was not much older when he married. Both marriages quickly brought children and responsibilities but later more or less failed (more in Dickens' case, less in Shakespeare's). Both writers fulfilled their responsibilities and were very aware of both family honour and the importance of money. There was to be no starving in a garret for either the great playwright or novelist, but a comfortable and respectable life in a good house with their children and parents well-provided for. This required constant hard work, so there could be no writer's block. Both men died in their fifties, worn out by their labours.

Shakespeare and Dickens both produced large amounts of work that brought great success and popularity during their lives, as well as considerable material comfort. They are the only writers in Britain who were loved by both the public of their day and by posterity. Neither enjoyed the advantages of a university education, aristocratic connections or a private income. Both became wealthy but neither lived to enjoy retirement. No-one doubts that Charles Dickens wrote Oliver Twist, yet the idea that someone was a stand-in for Shakespeare will not go away.

It is somehow unfair, therefore, that Shakespeare should have his achievements doubted and undermined. So how do you change the balance and not take away the credit he deserves? And should a guide even be involved or remain neutral in the authorship question? I believe he should be involved and should correct the misbalance of countless pseudo scholars who try to deny Shakespeare his rightful place. If nothing else, it seems a bit much to ask someone to pay forty or fifty pounds to go on a trip to Stratford if you do not even believe the man who lived there wrote anything worthwhile.

This is a test for a guide. In a sense it shows whether he is being serious about his job. It is easy to exploit a popular myth to gain a little attention on a slow day, to perpetuate a myth rather than explain the reality. No-one will die if we allow the lazy assumptions to flourish. The world will not stop spinning and the economy will not implode. People will still come to visit Stratford and many of them will see a play, even read a poem and some will be better off for it, while others will be merely puzzled.

But something will die if guides always take the lazy route. The gap between the academic and the lay person, already pretty wide, will grow a bit wider. The attitude that Shakespeare is hard for people, so we let us reduce him to a theme park curiosity, will grow a little stronger. People who are genuinely excited by the stars and the immensity of space must be annoyed by stories of alien abductions because they encourage us to approach the question by looking inwards rather than looking outwards. We cannot really see the stars if we think there are little green men ready to whisk us off our planet to take us there, and we cannot really appreciate Shakespeare unless we acknowledge him as a human being with many of the fears and vanities we possess. Yes, he was vain enough to have a coat of arms made up, fond of money and almost certainly unfaithful to his wife. No he was not a superman aristocrat who hid behind the name of some poor player while he laughed at us. He would not be worth reading or watching if he was, let alone travelling to Stratford to see his house and that of his wife Anne Hathaway.

Most tourists have little interest in arcane academic arguments and the minutiae of scholarly investigations that try to identify the Dark Lady of the sonnets or discuss whether Mr W H is a misprint for Henry Wriothesley, the name of Shakespeare's patron, the young Earl of

Southampton. And they are not convinced by sentences that begin "Virtually all scholars agree" or "No-one seriously questions Shakespeare's authorship". Tourists need common sense argument not academic analysis to correct the common misconceptions about Shakespeare. You can break these down into three simple arguments:

- **The Dickens Comparison**: Only some will have read George Eliot or D H Lawrence but most will have heard of Dickens and know the outline of Oliver Twist and David Copperfield. The two had similar backgrounds and were driven by the same demons. Both knew the value of popular success, a full house or a best-seller, and they were not afraid to use their talents to cash in, although neither really enjoyed much on the way of a retirement.

- **The Rural Context**: This will appeal to people who think of themselves as country people – quite a high proportion, even if they live in the suburbs. Shakespeare was not really a city person, although he left Stratford for London to make a success. Less than a thousand people lived in Stratford when he was alive and everybody relied on the countryside for a living in one way or another. This comes out in his knowledge of flowers and in the rhythms of rural life, making a living from the land. Ophelia's flowers and harvest in The Winter's Tale spring immediately to mind. That does not prove he was not an aristocrat but it does indicate an intimate knowledge of everyday life next to the land.

- **Twins:** This should clinch it for the doubters. Twins are important in Shakespeare. He was the father of twins, Judith and Hamnet, and they appear in two of his best known comedies. The Comedy of Errors was written in Shakespeare's early career when his son Hamnet was still alive. It involves two sets of twins mistaken for each other and the resulting confusion, eventually happily resolved with lovers and spouses reunited. It is a happy and undemanding play, a good introduction to Shakespeare for children. After Hamnet's death, however, he wrote Twelfth Night, which again features humour caused by the misidentification of twins. The difference in this play is that each twin thinks the other has died in the shipwreck, whereas in the earlier play they were separated at birth. This creates a much sadder play with some wonderful poetry of loss over laden with the irony of disguised sexual identification. Viola/ Cesario's speech to Orsino about his/her sister dying of grief was surely inspired by the fact that Shakespeare of Stratford had a twin daughter grieving her brother who had died three years earlier.

These are the lines:

My father had a daughter lov'd a man,
As it might be perhaps, were I a woman,
I should your lordship.

> *And what's her history?*

A blank, my lord, she never told her love,
But let concealment like a worm i' the bud,
Feed on her damask cheek: she pin'd in thought,
And with a green and yellow melancholy,
She sat like Patience on a monument,
Smiling at grief. Was not this love indeed?
We men say more, swear more; but indeed
Our shows are more than will, for still we prove
Much in our vows, but little in our love.

But died thy sister of her love, my boy?

I am all the daughters of my father's house

How can anyone hearing these beautiful lines not believe that Shakespeare was inspired to them by the loss of a son and the survival of a twin sister? That shaft of ice, of course, led him to use his loss to inspire his most tender play. He intended the irony to come from the truth of Viola's last line, that she is all the daughters of her father's house, a fact known to us but concealed from the Duke. Yet there is a further echo for us today in the fact that poor sad Judith, who could not sign her own name as an adult and broke her father's heart by marrying a useless chancer in her thirties, must have pined for her twin brother Hamnet who died when they were both twelve and Shakespeare was away in London working in the theatre and writing poems for the Earl of Southampton.

Conspiracy theorists cannot be persuaded out of their beliefs. They keep coming up with new and ever more improbable scenarios that fit their chosen explanation. When the conspiracy occurred not forty years ago, as in the case of Kennedy, but four hundred years ago, it is even harder to dissuade them. It is a free country – at least as far as Shakespeare is concerned – and no-one can disprove a negative. It is not impossible that Shakespeare's plays were written by someone else, just unthinkable. Yet, it would be good to think that tourist guides appreciated the real Shakespeare enough to take him away from the conspiracy theorists.

CHAPTER TEN:

ROYALIST OR REPUBLICAN?

Attitudes to monarchy

oyalty and tourist guiding are inextricably linked. A party on a full day tour of London sees the changing of the guard at Buckingham Place, visits Westminster Abbey where the Queen's ancestors are buried and where she was crowned, goes to St Paul's Cathedral where her son and Diana were married and then to the Tower, seeping with royal connections and regalia. On a 'non-royal' tour, which does not touch the subject directly – to Stonehenge and Bath, for example, or Stratford and Oxford – people will ask questions in the dead parts of the day when driving along the motorway and the future of royalty often comes up. Tourists from the USA and Europe have an outsider's fascination with the institution while those from the Commonwealth have closer links with the royal family, even if the continuation of these is under continuous discussion, as in Australia. While a qualified guide will know more about the history of royalty than a tourist, it is quite possible that members of his party will know more of the royal gossip. There is something sad but inevitable in the way the royal family have become the subject of this kind of journalism. The nineteenth century historian Walter Bagehot distinguished between the efficient and the dignified parts of the constitution - government was efficient, while royalty was dignified. The truth of the first part of that distinction is debatable while that of the second part has all but disappeared.

The questions people ask about the monarchy reflect the way that attitudes have changed over the years. In the late seventies and early eighties, when the royal family had approval ratings that politicians would kill for, the mood was one of what happens next? Questions tended to concentrate on when the Queen was going to "hand over" the throne to Prince Charles. Now all tourist guides are asked whether Charles will be bypassed in favour of his less sullied, more marketable son William. Both ideas are based on misapprehensions – the first that the role of a monarch was like a career with a pension plan and retirement date, the second that it was perfectly possible to skip a generation if the future holder was considered unsuitable, or just unlovable.

The trouble is that it *has* happened before. When Edward VIII did the unthinkable and fell in love with an American divorcee, he was shunted aside in favour his dutiful but nervous younger brother Albert, Duke of York, the Queen's father. Although he officially abdicated in favour of George VI, everyone knew that he wanted both Wallis Simpson and the crown but had to choose between the two. Most of the establishment, who regarded him as dangerously independent and unstable, were relieved that he chose her. It could be argued that the royal family and those who supported its continuation had good reason to be grateful to the Baltimore divorcee for taking a man with a weakness for Hitler's style of government away from the centre of power. Not that they showed any gratitude to her – the Duke and Duchess of Windsor were not invited to the Queen's coronation and her existence was only grudgingly acknowledged at the Duke's funeral.

Once the rules have been changed, it is hard to unchange them and go back to a rigidly inflexible system. In fact, the system of royal inheritance was never that inflexible. Long civil wars were fought in both the twelfth and fifteenth centuries over the succession and the second of these was brought to an end by the simple expedient of Henry Tudor winning a battle, killing his rival and marrying into the opposition's family. In 1485, after the bloodletting of the Wars of the Roses, he was the only credible male still standing and had relatively little opposition in establishing his dubious right to rule.

Henry VII's capture of the crown (supposedly found in a hawthorn bush) has little direct relevance to the position of Prince Charles but it does demonstrate that the British royal family has always had a hint of expediency about it. Unsuitable or unpopular kings have been dispatched in the past, either privately in the case of the unworldly Henry VI, or publicly as in the inflexible and vain Charles I. A tour of London will see where both men were killed – Henry was murdered in the Wakefield Tower in the Tower of London and Charles was executed at Horse Guard's Parade in Whitehall, his death commemorated with a solemn parade every year on the last Sunday in January. A visit to Windsor sees where Edward VIII made his abdication broadcast. Most people will be more interested in the visually striking sights in these places - crown jewels, mounted soldiers, royal apartments – but it is worth pointing them out to show that Charles can take nothing for granted.

The best way to put his prospects is in the form of a double negative: it is unlikely that he will fail to succeed. His mistakes are those of trying too hard to do the right thing and then finding he did not have the heart to follow it through. He has been the opposite of Edward VIII who married for love - and hang the consequences. Charles married for duty and could be forgiven. His mother comes from a line of long-lived women and, having reached fifty years, seems determined to see it through to the end instead of taking the European option of retirement through abdication. His reign will probably be short and, if he can control his tendency to talk without thinking, sensible rather than glorious.

What is the alternative? To skip to William would be unthinkable if royalty is to be taken seriously as an institution. What if he lost the popularity he has built up through little more than good looks and avoiding controversy? What if he did not want to go straight to the throne when his grandmother dies but would like to enjoy a period of relative obscurity before succeeding? Would there be an opinion poll or an election to find who was the most popular member of the royal family? What future is there anyway for what seems like an anachronistic institution in an egalitarian meritocratic age? The fact that there are so many question marks in this paragraph shows how flexible our relationship with royalty is. Little can be taken for granted and the royal establishment feels that it is best to change as little and as slowly as possible to avoid becoming tied up in the kind of celebrity culture which is so fickle.

Where does the tourist guide fit into this discussion? There is no official line for guides to take on royalty, but what we might call guidelines are probably advisable. Generally speaking, it is not a good idea for a guide to put over a strong personal point of view when conducting a tour. This may seem unfair, but think about it for a moment. You, a tourist, have paid to see a particular city or site, you are expecting to hear information about it, hopefully delivered in a lively style with the kind of insights you cannot find in a guidebook, you take your seat and then have to listen to someone putting forward his own opinions, which you have neither the chance nor the inclination to argue with. You are hardly likely to be very happy with the tour or the guide. Moreover, there is a natural and healthy inclination for people to reject ideas that are being force fed to them and the cause being espoused will probably suffer more than it will gain from relentless promotion. Politics might crop up but they can be dealt with as the Any Other Business of a tour when people start to ask questions and probe the guide for his views.

They will want to see a guide who is a living, thinking human being and inevitably he will have views on some topics. In practice, he will be more likely to get away with airing these if they are of a conservative rather than a radical nature because they would be more likely to coincide with those of most of his passengers. However, it is an area to be tiptoed through. A guide can usually indicate where he stands without forcing his opinions on his passengers.

It is impossible to ignore the royal family, however. While there is no obligation on guides to support the institution, it might seem that it is in their best interests to do so. No-one would lose their badge for openly criticising the Queen on a tour, but it might not be described as a good career move. Some guides are republican by conviction and may have difficulty in concealing their opinions. Others are unashamedly royalist and proud of it. In the period after the Queen's golden jubilee the issue is alive in a way that it was not around the silver jubilee, when republicanism was something of a joke, the preserve of one eccentric Labour MP, Willie Hamilton. Hamilton, an old fashioned Scottish socialist, would not rise very far in the New Labour hierarchy, but in his day he held a certain lonely dignity in his refusal to conform to political expediency.

Today republicanism is on the agenda in a way that it was not during Hamilton's time. Then, survival for the royal family depended on simply showing up for work with a pleasant demeanour and a bland acceptance of political neutrality. The Queen does not even vote, being above party politics. Her involvement in any issue is the equivalent of a raised eyebrow or, at most, a sharp intake of breath when confronted with a particularly divisive policy, especially if it could have a negative impact on her beloved Commonwealth. A close and stable family life, a sense of duty and an ability not to offend were enough to ensure royal continuance.

Now, something more is needed. Tradition alone is not enough to ensure an institution's survival in a time of change. Succession by birth rather than popular choice is at least questionable in an otherwise meritocratic system and there might seem to be no justification for a monarchy when other countries survive without one and when it wields no power. Those in favour of retaining the royal family have to meet the intellectual challenge of republicanism rather than just rely on inertia to preserve the institution.

So here goes.

When he made his series of programmes on Westminster Abbey for the BBC some years ago Alan Bennett quoted the historian Macaulay, who said that, "If it is not necessary to change, it is necessary not to change". Vic, an elderly Australian tourist, gave the modern version of this dictum when, asked why he had voted against his country becoming a republic, he replied, "If it ain't broke, don't fix it." Bennett's programmes, incidentally, were a wonderful example of guiding at its best - detailed, humane, witty and learned. No-one who was interested in history or architecture could fail to be impressed by them and many of us watching these programmes must have thought what a good guide Bennett would make. (I dare say he has other plans.)

This is not unthinking traditionalism, but sceptical conservatism. Of course, plenty of people, in both Britain and Australia, think that royalty is broke and needs fixing or replacing, but the onus is on them to prove that what they have to replace it with will make a material improvement in our everyday lives. Can anyone imagine British teams winning more world cups if the teams sang, say, "Let the republic flourish" instead of "God save the Queen" before games? Can anyone imagine British people having semi-spontaneous street parties or massive public celebrations after twenty five or fifty years of a republic, as they did for the silver and golden jubilees of Elizabeth?

It will, however, take more than the excuse of a good party to preserve the royal family. Their existence as a soap opera cast seems safer than as a part of Bagehot's dignified constitution. Divorces and disillusioned daughters-in-law, murder plots and dangerous dogs, dubious sexuality and parentage – all in the middle of enormous wealth and privilege: a scriptwriter might have difficulty selling some of these storylines to the most down-market television producers. It certainly makes a change from obsequiousness and over praise, but it does mean that the greater threat to the monarchy comes from within. As a moderately sympathetic outsider you wonder whether it can all be worth it. Maybe in a few generations the institution will fade away and eventually die as those within it decide to preserve their sanity rather than their status.

For most people, from Britain or abroad, this would be a shame. We enjoy royalty as one of those things that we do not really need but actually quite like, like cricket, afternoon tea and free art galleries. There are constitutional arguments both for and against having a monarchy. However, the truth is probably that the political life of this country would be little different without a monarch, although the chance of a totalitarian government coming to power is always greater in a republic than in a country where the loyalty of the armed forces and public servants is to the crown rather than the state.

It is in the small things that royalty makes a difference. Virtually every visitor to London, foreign or British, wants to see the Changing of the Guard. It is the poor person's visit to an art gallery or museum. It is free and it is fun. It is also an important part of a guide's repertoire: mess that up and you lose your tour. Yet, how could we keep it going without a royal family? Certainly, the Queen is often away from Buckingham Palace when the guards and their band march along the Mall, but even the British love of tradition would balk at paying trained soldiers to wear colourful and expensive costumes to guard a permanently empty building. If we are to say to the children and grandchildren of today's visitors that they cannot see the Changing of the Guard anymore, we have to have a good reason to give them for why it is no longer there. Telling them that it makes them somehow more equal with their fellow countrymen is unlikely to work.

In any case, the argument that egalitarianism is easier in a republic simply does not stand up to scrutiny. When Britain last had a Labour government, long before New Labour was conceived, we enjoyed some of the highest income tax rates in the free world, outdone only by a few

Scandinavian countries, several of which are also monarchies. No diaries of ministers of the time ever so much as hint that the Queen or any other member of the royal family stood in the way of these high rates of personal taxation. (They did not have to because none of the royals then paid tax.) The royal assent was not withheld from the finance bills that brought in these progressive rates of taxation – in fact, it is three hundred years since this prerogative was last used – and British people paid up more or less uncomplainingly.

Contrast this with the United States, where they have had a republic for over two hundred years, and you will find far more regressive rates of taxation. It is an interesting exercise to tell passengers how much tax we pay in Britain. While our tax levels are now fairly standard for a European democracy, almost all Americans think that they are too high, and that the rates imposed by what they would classify as socialist administrations in the sixties and seventies were punitive. If you really want to see their jaws drop tell them about the ninety eight per cent tax rates for investment income brought in by Old Labour.

It was not a Queen anxious to protect privilege and extend inequality who ended these tax rates, it was the people. Labour today will do anything to avoid being seen as a high taxing egalitarian party because they know it would be the kiss of death for their electoral prospects. If socialism is to be re-attempted in Britain, a highly dubious prospect in the kind of innovative and flexible economy full of self-employed people and short-term contracts that we now have, it will not be the presence or absence of royalty that makes it possible. It will be the contest between greed and idealism, one that idealism seems to be losing badly at present.

In fact, you could go further and say that, in a curious way, the royal family is actually a kind of socialist institution. Everyone pays for it, through their taxes, and everyone can enjoy it. While some people do not go to university or to hospital, others do not drive cars or claim benefit, everyone can go along to Buckingham Palace and see the Changing of the Guard. Try it some time. The best place to start is probably at St James's Palace at around eleven o'clock in the morning (every day in high summer, alternate days for the rest of the year). From there you follow the guards up the Mall to the Palace and see a larger troop and its band arriving at eleven thirty. After that it is half an hour of jostling for position and children climbing on shoulders to get a decent view before the guards come out at noon, again accompanied by their band. Everyone should do that at least once in his or her life, preferably before cynicism sets in. Take your children and then tell them that they would really be better off in a republic.

If we were starting from scratch, as many English speaking countries did two hundred years ago, we would probably not design a monarchy into our system. But there is something about the British character that is rightly suspicious of people hurrying towards perfection through the abolition of ancient institutions. There have been many examples of these turning into murderous tyrannies in the living memory in places like Cambodia, Germany or Russia, but maybe it is better to look backwards rather than outwards to find an example of our own.

It is often forgotten (or ignored) when discussions about royalty come up, but England has been a republic. The experiment lasted for just over eleven years from Charles I's execution in January 1649 to the restoration of the monarchy a year and a half after Oliver Cromwell's death in September 1658. Cromwell had many abilities but there would have been few who would have voted for a continuation of his Commonwealth experiment when Charles II returned from exile in 1660, caustically remarking that he would not have stayed away so long if he had known that he would be welcomed home so enthusiastically.

All schoolchildren know that the puritans abolished Christmas and dancing around the maypole. Charles I may have a pretty dreadful king, inflexible without being

142

inspirational, but people could at least have some fun under his rule. Fun was pretty much forbidden under Cromwell and it is one of the tragedies of English history that his fellow leader of the parliamentary army, Lord Fairfax, was never able to assume power and marry democracy with monarchy. Instead Cromwell became Lord Protector, effectively dictator, and was even offered the crown, which he refused after much deliberation. At least he wins some respect for maintaining his integrity in this refusal and in his strict and simple lifestyle while in power. What he did not win was the hearts of the people, ruling through fear and might rather than by consent. He failed to create a system that was accepted by the people and, the greatest irony of all, attempted to pass power to his own son Richard, who had neither the inclination nor the ability to assume it. Cromwell senior's body was disinterred and hung twelve years to the day after Charles I's execution at Whitehall, while Cromwell junior was left to live in retirement.

Despite this unsubtle degradation of the Cromwellian corpse and the execution of the other still living regicides, the restoration of the monarchy was a remarkably un-brutal affair. The fact that Cromwell's son and heir and his brother Henry were left alone to live out their lives in peace after their father's state collapsed says a great deal about a spirit of forgiveness for which the restored monarch Charles must take some credit. He could be ruthless and disloyal when he needed to be but seemed to have a generous enough spirit to avoid merely vindictive bloodshed.

Even more surprising was the toleration shown to John Milton, the blind poet who lived in Cripplegate just a few miles from Whitehall. There, in perpetual darkness with the long-suffering women who looked after him and acted as his scribes and readers (without being allowed to understand a word of the ancient texts they were reading) Milton composed Paradise Lost. Instead of keeping a discreet distance from his former leader, Milton refused to moderate his views and published hardline republican pamphlets even as the monarchy was returning in 1659-60.

The language of Paradise Lost is full of kingly references but few of them are flattering, and in the very first book there is an allusion to recent events in England;

> *When the sun new risen*
> *Looks through the horizontal misty air*
> *Shorn of his beams, or from behind the moon*
> *In dim eclipse disastrous twilight sheds*
> *On half the nations, and with fear of change*
> *Perplexes monarchs.*

This may be a reference to Cromwell as the moon, obscuring the sun, the symbol of kingship, causing consternation to those who believed that kings were appointed by God to rule over men. Whatever the symbolism behind this passage, the language used makes it obvious where Milton's sympathies lie. No royalist, or even a diplomatic republican, would use a phrase like 'perplexes monarchs'. His blindness seemed to make him unwilling to acknowledge the existence of the danger of what he was writing. Despite this, Milton was left in peace and died a natural death to be buried next to his father in St Giles' Church, set somewhat incongruously amidst the high rise towers of the Barbican in the middle of the City of London.

Compare this to the treatment in France of Antoine Lavoisier a century later. Lavoisier was a brilliant chemist and made many advances in science which are still considered important today. Like many of the thinkers of the day he was a gentleman scholar rather a professional academic – such men hardly existed at the time. He made a living by being a tax collector, or tax farmer as it was then known, and a certain amount of creative accountancy was considered necessary for men of this profession. This assumption did him little good after the revolution in Paris, however, and he became one of many victims of the guillotine simply because of his means of income. According to popular myth, he asked for a short stay of execution when he learned of his fate, as he wished to finish some experiments. The judge refused his request saying that the new republic had no need of scientists. If the arrogant and brutal new French republic had no need of science, then the restored England monarchy certainly had no use for an openly republican poet who refused to hide his beliefs. Yet the poet lived and the chemist was killed.

Does the fate of a stubborn poet and an elegant chemist have any relevance to the republican movement of today and to tourist guiding? I think so. Republicanism is for people who want everything to be the same, for all systems to be organised logically rather to adapt and evolve through tradition and usage. At its most harmless, this is merely dull. At its most aggressive it becomes tyrannical and frightening as large reorganisations of society by the Khmer Rouge or Mao's cultural warriors proved to be. Tourist guiding is about relating the past to the present and celebrating the differences between countries rather than promoting homogenous and uniform systems of government.

Tony Blair put a rare foot wrong when he encouraged people to come from abroad to see Britain's modern achievements such as the Millennium Dome. People in Seattle and Sydney do not lack new buildings of their own and have no need to spend thousands of dollars and weeks in travelling to see our rather tame skyscratchers. It is Windsor Castle and Buckingham Palace that can only be seen here. These places are not only part of our physical landscape but of our national identity. They are what make Britain individual and different. They are why people get onto an aeroplane, to see what they do not have at home. They appreciate our history even more if it can be seen to have survived and adapted to the present day.

There is, of course, a difference between preserving the past and living in it. Charles I lost his throne because he was unable or unwilling to adapt to the changing times and insisted on clinging to the outdated notion of the divine right of kings to rule over people. By adapting to the demands of greater democracy, from the restoration onwards, royalty has maintained a link with the people of Britain. The rate of change has been accelerating in recent years and the royal establishment now more often seems to be following rather than leading when it comes to innovation. At the time of the Queen's silver jubilee in 1977 there was an unmistakable spontaneity and affection in the way that people celebrated the event. The golden jubilee was a more muted affair and the big concerts at Buckingham Palace, although packed out, had more the air of being organised from the top down rather the bottom up, unlike the street parties that people enjoyed in the wet summer twenty five years earlier. Similarly, the suggested change in the royal line of succession now involves bypassing Charles rather than going straight to him with the Queen stepping down to spend more time with her corgis.

What happened in between to cause this change in attitude? Diana, the late Princess of Wales, stands beside any discussion of the royal family, just as Oliver Cromwell lurks behind it. There is something ironic in the fact that Cromwell, a determined and ruthless man with a clear vision of what he wanted to achieve, failed to rid Britain of its link with royalty, while she almost succeeded. Without any academic qualifications and with no anti-royal agenda, she did more than anyone else to undermine its foundations. What were her motivations? She never seemed to have more than a personal agenda which grew out of her own understandable frustrations with the family she had entered but which she did not feel welcome in. Diana never made any promises to republican movements and did not even seem to support converting the Windsors to a more relaxed Scandinavian style of monarchy. None of us would have taken much notice of Lady Diana Spencer if she had not become Princess Di. She gained all her fame through the path of marriage into a family she came to hate and then seemed to want to destroy that family. Could this be described as biting the hand that feeds you?

Now Diana criticism is even more unthinkable than

Queen criticism on a tour. She undoubtedly had, whatever her failings in logical consistency, great star quality and huge charisma. The royal family have generally been stronger on duty than charisma and could have done with absorbing that quality in a way that did not damage their standing. However, if there is to be a choice between dutiful conscientious plodding and brilliant but unpredictable charisma, the former is probably a better long-term asset than the latter. There is an echo here of the Duke of Windsor, who in later years was inclined to grumble about how he had been treated by his country "after all he had done for it", just as Diana was resentful of her in-laws and their treatment of her.

The royals decided they could do without her help in the end and she was virtually expelled from their ranks from the time of her notorious Panorama interview with the BBC until her death. This was the lowest point for royalty in Britain when the Windsors were seen to be callous and self-serving. Yet in some way, the royal family was actually stronger after Diana's death. None of those who left flowers at Kensington Palace really wanted a republic. They wanted to enjoy both Diana's charisma and the Windsor's longevity, even though the two were in conflict. Indifference would have been more of a threat than this essentially short-term partisanship caused by taking sides in a family row.

Diana could have been a brilliant asset to royalty but the deal somehow did not work. She just did not like the reality of life with them. It became fashionable to refer to the royal family as being dysfunctional when things started to go wrong with the marriages of the Queen's children. Yet surely the problem was that the Windsor family was over functional rather than dysfunctional. Everything worked perfectly well in their households until young and lively women joined them and found their routines stultifying. If Charles had been prepared to break away from his parents a little more he might have stood a better chance of hitting it off with young wife. She became bored by Balmoral and all the other large houses where routines had continued unbroken for decades.

Diana is a memory now, almost as harmless as the Duke and Duchess of Windsor, unless a new murder theory pops up. The royal family survives and so does tourism. Helping guides to make a living is not in itself justification for keeping royalty going. As the Conservative MP Anne Widdecombe said during a debate on fox-hunting in Parliament, abolishing crime would ultimately put police officers out of work, but that is no reason not to try. Nevertheless there is something to be said for longevity. Put simply, royalty is one of the things we do in Britain. We do it well, in the way that we do not do making motor cars or televisions.

In some countries the guide is obliged to support and espouse the government point of view and will lose his job if he fails to do so. That, fortunately, is not the case in Britain, where people are free to hold and espouse any views they want. So, guides can be republicans if they choose. It just seems a little like turkeys voting for Christmas.

CHAPTER ELEVEN:
CHURCH GOING
Guiding in churches, attending services

I was in church when I first decided to become a guide. Actually, that is misleading. I was in a church but I was not worshipping and was in no position to decide on future employment prospects, being twelve and with no idea of what I wanted to do when I grew up. The church was Chartres Cathedral and we were on a family holiday, one of several we took each summer in a series of battered second hand cars, at least one of which never made it back to Britain. "Seen Naples and died" my brothers and I wrote on the dust of the back of one of them, a mobster-like Triumph Standard that had room for all seven of us.

The guide at Chartres was Malcolm Miller, probably Britain's best known tourist guide, although I doubt if he ever conducted tours in this country. He stayed in Chartres during the summer and conducted two tours a day around the cathedral for anyone who showed up. There was no set charge for the tour and people were invited to join as it progressed around the church. Then at the end he made a little speech about money and people paid if they wanted to. The system obviously worked for Miller and he seemed to make a comfortable amount twice a day.

We went into plenty of churches and galleries on these improving holidays and I would be lying if I said we approached the task enthusiastically. My parents planned the itineraries and my father, brought up in South Africa with little immediate contact with European culture, was anxious to make up for lost time. My brothers and I went along with varying degrees of enthusiasm. However, I was entranced by Miller's performance and, being at an impressionable age, it obviously planted a seed which sprouted much later. By that time, a dozen years afterwards, I was sitting at a Civil

Service desk, bored and underused, and went back to the idea of becoming a guide. It took some time but I have never looked back. I have been disappointed and frustrated plenty of times since, but rarely bored again.

What I took from Miller that day in Chartres was the value of staying fresh. If I had to define the secret of tourist guiding in a sentence I would say that it is saying the same thing over and over again and making it sound like it is the first time you have ever said it. Not, of course, because you stumble over the words but because you are interested in them, as if you have just made a fascinating discovery. As I have said earlier (guides always repeat the important things) it is the freshness that people respond to. The biggest danger is in becoming the air steward type of guide, repeating the words by rote without showing any expression or enthusiasm.

Miller's technique was to vary the tour each time. He knew every carving, statue and window of the cathedral so well that he could start with the same generalised introduction and then move to a different specialised example. He seemed to be saying that no two of his tours were ever the same, a good selling point which encouraged you to go back again.

I did go back, but it was twenty years before I returned to Chartres. Miller was still there and we went on his tour. I was with my girlfriend, who was French, also a guide, and we were a little more detached - two professionals eying up another, looking for faults maybe. I had heard from a friend that Miller could be very temperamental if you did not do things his way and that he made little secret of his intolerance for guided tours that were here today and gone tomorrow. He was definitely the scholarly type of guide rather than the schmaltzy type and would probably have been a disaster with a group over an extended period.

Yet I still enjoyed his tour the second time around. Chartres is a curiously untouched, almost homogenous church. Most British cathedrals have been buffeted over the centuries by the forces of nature and of human conflict.

Hitler and Cromwell, the reformation and erosion have all forced numerous rebuildings on our oldest churches until they may be unrecognisable to those who put them there in the first place. The most common question people have of a church, or any other major building, is "When was it built"? This can be a difficult one to answer as there may be nothing of the original left and most of what you see would have been constructed long after the building was envisaged.

Chartres, on the other hand, was built in a relatively short time and was never bombed, burnt or defaced by religious reformers. Well-preserved, largely unaltered and with a wealth of gothic detail but no major tombs or monuments to distract you from the building itself, it is virtually pure architecture. This makes it a godsend for a guide like Miller who took the time to study every inch of the church and familiarise himself not only with the decoration but the provenance, the background of who was responsible for each section and the significance of each symbol to them.

It was very touching the way that long-dead merchants were brought back to life by this twentieth century scholar and guide, their carefully budgeted gifts explained with care and love to a mostly sceptical audience. Sceptical not so much of the building, but of the faith behind it. Replacing the almost universal confidence in (or fear of) the afterlife that existed when Chartres was built is a vague hope that death does not bring complete extinction. If there is something after life, if not the afterlife that the Chartres donors envisaged, then it will occur for people whether they worship or not. Their visits to places like Chartres are almost always to find out more about this world rather than the next one.

I have another vivid church memory from guiding, or rather from preparing for guiding. I had decided to try and enter the profession but was still tied to a desk in Waterloo. I crossed the river one lunchtime and went into Westminster Abbey armed with a Michelin guidebook to investigate. Half an hour later I remember sitting down in the nave completely convinced that the attempt was hopeless. I would never understand enough about this building to be able to take people around it. There were simply too many tombs, statues and chapels to take in. Later, of course, I came to understand that many of the approximately two thousand people buried in the Abbey are of little importance and that their tombs can safely be ignored. The royal tombs, the poets, politicians and scientists, all conveniently congregated together by profession, can be pointed out easily enough with references to the coronation chair and ceremony, the architecture and history of the building.

The Abbey, not a cathedral but our most interesting national church, is also used for worship every day of the year, not just on Sundays. Sightseers far outnumber worshippers, of course. Britain is a country which has some of the finest churches in the world combined with one of the lowest rates of attendance at service. Indeed, when we were discussing safety procedures at Westminster Abbey some years ago, a deacon said ruefully that the best way to empty the church in a hurry was to announce that a service was about to begin. People would soon make their way out rather than be trapped inside to take part in the activity for which the building had been designed.

This sort of resigned humour is not uncommon amongst people who work in churches, which are used to small congregations of elderly regulars followed by massive influxes of tourists coming to look and photograph rather than worship. The regulars sometimes seem more at home in the church than their own houses, while the occasionals make a lot of noise but do not linger. It must seem like the army – long periods of boredom followed by massive bursts of frenzy as churches struggle to contain the crowds.

On the whole, churches welcome people whatever the motive for their visit. They know that the majority of visitors may not be regulars, but that they are enough in touch with the church to respect the building. The men take off their hats and put away their cameras if asked to do so and they generally make a donation in the box if encouraged by example or exhortation. This money can be very important for the church and they have developed increasingly determined methods of extracting it.

Donations given on entering a church are not subject to Value Added Tax, while entrance fees are. They are also a very uncertain way of raising funds for the maintenance of old buildings. People usually give if prompted but most get rid of loose change at best if left to their own devices. Sometimes they are positively defiant about not giving, as though the church should be above such matters. One of the most mean-spirited comments I have ever read in a visitors' book criticised Wells Cathedral for asking for donations: "They are more interested in our money than anything else." No they aren't. They would love to save your soul as well, but they need to keep the building up to do that and will not do so from freeloaders, those who come to look but do not pay. They exist in Caesar's world and need to have funds rendered to survive in it.

Fed up and under funded by relying on visitors' unprompted generosity, many cathedrals have developed a system of 'enhanced donations'. These are entrance fees by any other name. Salisbury Cathedral pioneered this system and others have followed. An entrance gate is installed and a 'suggested donation' sign is put up. Someone waits at the gate and supervises your donation, even giving change and possibly issuing a ticket to the visitor. The legal fig leaf of volunteering is observed while the moral pressure to pay is quite apparent – and effective. The church gets its money without having to surrender any of it back to the government.

Malcolm Miller could afford to rely on the generosity of his audience, although it was not unprompted. Those who chose not to pay him were an insignificant number and almost certainly fewer than those who would be put off by having to pay in advance. He, however, was providing a show and was considered good value. Spiritual uplift was secondary (and far away for my twelve year old self). Although he was always gracious in acceptance and evidently loved his work, the money for Miller was an end. For the church it was a means. They needed it to stay open, in some cases to stay upright.

This is probably why Salisbury was the pioneer of the enhanced donation system. Built on a marsh eight hundred years ago it has a smallish congregation in a city of 50,000 people already well-endowed with parish churches that have financial pressures of their own. Christopher Wren, who was born nearby, had put up some support arches in the seventeenth century but the weight of Britain's tallest church pressing down on some of its shallowest foundations for seven and a half centuries was making the tower of the church buckle and the spire sway gently, about half an inch ever year. The church needed money to correct this and to restore its famous west front. It was not getting enough from the tourists.

If anything, the erosion and undermining of the cathedral was being aggravated rather than ameliorated by large numbers of coach parties stopping for an hour or so. A cathedral like Salisbury will welcome a six or even seven figure number of visitors a year. Most have just come down from Stonehenge where they had already spent much of their money in the gift shop and many just take a photograph or two before wandering into town. The cathedral wanted its share of the tourist dollar and began to implement a strategy to harvest it.

Who can blame them? Certainly not the tour companies, many of which regularly mention cathedrals in their itineraries without costing in an entrance fee. They like cathedrals because they are attractive old buildings which do not cost them anything. The cathedrals in turn have become wise to this and have developed strategies to cash in on their value. No longer can you expect to wander into one and raise your eyes heavenwards past the soaring arches - without first digging into your pockets to pay your three or four pounds (less for pensioners).

Sometimes the press of tourists becomes simply too much and the church feels that groups have to be discouraged from entering. This happened in Westminster Abbey when Wesley Carr was appointed Dean in 1995. He took one look at the massive crush of tour groups going through every morning and decided that enough was enough. He effectively introduced a congestion charge for groups by limiting their size and restricting the area in which guides could address them. This was called "Reclaiming the Calm" and was greeted less than enthusiastically by London blue badge guides, who did not care to have their tours abridged. Groups would generally go to the Abbey immediately before driving up Whitehall to see the Changing of the Guard which made for high concentrations of people and decibels between nine and eleven in the morning. After Reclaiming the Calm group numbers dropped rapidly, especially as tourist numbers generally were going down at the time. The Abbey suddenly found it was short of funds and looked to attract more visitors, although they did not go as far as reversing their new policy. They soon learned that they could not have it both ways – tourists bring problems but they also bring cash.

Most cathedrals compete with each other to attract paying visitors. And they do not just court the tourist. Film and television companies are equally if not more welcome, not only for the fees they themselves bring, but for the knock-on effect that the film location has in attracting more visitors. This has led to a growth in an odd kind of tourism, seeing something not for what it is but because of what it is disguised as. Whole areas of Yorkshire, a county supposedly more sure of its own identity than any other, profit considerably from the fact that television companies use them for making fictional series. These programmes are often geographically loyal to the source area but set in a time around thirty to fifty years ago when golden age criteria come into effect. Roads were less crowded, neighbours more conversational and even the weather was better (or more spectacularly bad). The implied message was that people were just much nicer in our parents' and grandparents' day so anywhere which can still look like it did when they were young has the potential to cash in.

Up until recently I was able to avoid television tourism, except maybe as an incidental on a general tour, like showing the old Port of London Authority building by the Tower to British groups and saying that it was used in The Professionals series (sad and dated, I know). James Bond is always good for a few remarks on locations, particularly after MI6 allowed their Vauxhall building to be used and a boat chase along the River Thames was in a pre-credit sequence (still the Dome's finest hour). It is always fraught with problems, in any case, because the more the passenger knows about a programme the more he is likely to be disappointed in the gap between real and filmed images. This reached its ultimate absurdity when I took the trouble to find the house in Coventry used in the television series Keeping up Appearances. We even stopped the coach to ask the local milkman but, when we got there, the anorak who had wanted to see it only remarked that "it didn't look anything like what he had expected". The set dressers had been and gone and the illusion had vanished.

Then along came Harry Potter to bring people back into cathedrals once again - Durham and Gloucester Cathedrals to be precise. These were used in the first two Potter films and, although their appearances were fleeting and confined to backdrops, it did bring in plenty of people in the summer of 2002 when tours based on the Harry Potter films suddenly started selling very well. These tourists, however, were not always welcome. Although it is pretty harmless stuff for most people, you have to be something of a spiritual and intellectual contortionist to make J K Rowling's magic and wizardry compatible with Christianity. There are a few of those in the Church of England but there are also those who dislike the way their churches seemed to have sold out to Hollywood and attracted parties of American children accompanied by indulgent parents and grandparents looking for Hogwart's school.

At what stage does the purpose of a church become incompatible with its need to raise money to survive? Harry Potter tourism did not undermine the church but it did receive a few sniffy looks from some churchgoers. On the whole they feel that the benefits usually outweigh the annoyance - but some of them took a lot more convincing this time. This was particularly as the kids looking for Hogwart's were only interested in the church because of its role as a film set. Unless tightly controlled they would run around, not take of their baseball caps and generally enjoy themselves.

Now that is not considered either unusual or reprehensible in itself, just not right for the inside of a nine hundred year old place of worship - inappropriate, to use the fashionable, and in this case accurate, word. Entering a church might not bring about instant salvation or conversion but it does sometimes induce a little hush of thoughtfulness of the kind Philip Larkin experienced in his poem Church Going. He enters with his bicycle clips still on, prepared to sneer at the ordinariness and redundancy of the place but stays to reflect on the value such places still have for atheists like himself.

Larkin's frowsty barn is an unknown empty parish church rather the kind of cathedral that still attracts large crowds of tourists. The Irish sixpence he leaves will hardly pay for the new roof it needs and the church would have (maybe already has) been closed because of a lack of regular worshippers. Sceptics like the poet do not keep a church going, even if they keep going to churches. Those who are prepared to put aside their doubts, or have none, show up every Sunday and justify its continuing as a living building. Occasionally, on Harry Potter days, they do not like 'their' building being invaded but more often they welcome people in, hoping that they might have a Larkinesque moment.

Churches often have an hourly prayer when guides stop their tours and listen while the prayer is made from the pulpit, usually with a microphone to sound above the buzz of guides and groups jostling. The din of a large number of tourists in a confined space all trying to hear what their guide has to say dies down, the prayer is completed, the Lord's Prayer follows, people mumble along, 'Amen' sounds and the din resumes. It is like an engine stalling and restarting: Oh, we are having a prayer. Quiet please, sit or kneel if you like for a minute. Now, let's go on to the next monument or tomb.

Most guides realise that this pause for prayer means something to the people in their group, a reminder of what the building is for, a connection with its past. In some groups people begin to pray themselves. A guide should never underestimate the religious sensibilities of those in his group. While few British people go to church regularly and almost all drink alcohol, this is inverted in many parts of the USA, where for many people churchgoing, teetotalism and conservative values go together. These are likely to provide a high proportion of those who buy a coach tour and they will not be responsive to any guide who does not respect their religious views.

Respect and agreement are not the same. A guide should be able to leave (and sometimes arrange for) his passengers to worship in peace even if he does not share their sympathies. He will probably be invited to join the kind of group prayers that often precede a day's outing. This can be one of those critical moments which make or break a tour, where even the body language used can be critical for the guide's relationship with his party. A dismissive refusal could alienate a party, while a polite one should not. Maybe a little tactful hypocrisy would do no harm. So, say that you have urgent business checking luggage if you cannot bear the thought of praying, or go along to the service and sit quietly at the back – you are unlikely to be expected to start speaking in tongues.

Some parties coming from the USA are looking for religious roots, particularly if they are Methodists. Methodism was born in England and, although it is moribund in many areas here, it still thrives in parts of the states, particularly in the south. There is a certain Methodist route that guides who are planning to conduct extended tours should familiarise themselves with. It starts at Epworth in Lincolnshire where John and Charles Wesley were born. The party will find out about their formidable mother Susanna, who many consider the real founder of the church, and then move on to Lincoln College in Oxford, where John studied and taught, possibly to Bristol, where he built his first church, and to the Methodist chapel in Moorgate St, London, where he is buried. It was in Oxford that the word Methodism came about as a description of the sect of worthy, high-minded young men who lived a methodical and rigorous lifestyle with, the implication goes, little time for fun or frivolity. It is one of those words like gothic and Tory that started as a term of abuse and ended up being a mark of pride.

Certainly Methodists would pride themselves on being upright citizens today. They tend to be socially and politically conservative, abstemious and full of bonhomie, sometimes to the point of being platitudinous. George Bush Junior and Margaret Thatcher are both Methodists and yet so too is Nelson Mandela, so there is no automatic equivalence between the faith and political conservatism. Baptists are in a similar vein, with a greater emphasis on moral purity and teetotalism. Guides need to be careful about making jokes about or references to alcohol in their company.

While many Americans have a tendency towards religion and abstinence, the opposite is the case with people from Australia. Despite, or because of, their delight in beating what they still think of as the mother country at almost any sport invented, Australians share a lot of the social and cultural assumptions of the British. They generally mistrust teetotallers, are sceptical of religiosity and are much more interested in what they can see and touch than what they cannot. Although it is less common now, you often used to hear them complaining about an ABC tour – "Another Bloody Cathedral".

The pious, the indifferent and the curious can all be found on the same tour. It is best to avoid dragging people into buildings that they do not want to visit, so I try whenever possible to provide alternatives to church going. There is usually a shopping area near the cathedral so people can rejoin the group later and they might even hear that the rest of the group had enjoyed the visit.

This is, frankly, less likely to happen if you hand over to a guide in the church. Bless them, local and church guides have very different priorities to tour directors with large parties and limited time and the two sometimes come into not always dignified conflict. Guides who only conduct tours of one building usually know its every detail and cannot resisting passing these on. Give them the chance and they will use every minute of your time (and more) to explain these, often to people whose absorption levels have long since been exceeded and who are keen to just stop listening to someone (anyone) for a while. Guides taking groups on an extended tour around Britain cannot know every church the group passes but being able to do a half hour tour of, say, York Minster which shows all the main features of the building is very useful. People will appreciate the extra hour it leaves them to walk down the Shambles and on to the Viking Museum.

The other alternative is to go to a service there. This can be surprisingly successful if handled properly, despite the comment of the Westminster deacon. Every cathedral in Britain has a daily evensong service, whether or not anyone from outside attends. . It is a non-communion service, so there is no problem with people from other churches attending, and it consists of readings, prayers and anthems such as the Nunc Dimitis. This usually takes place around five in the afternoon (earlier on Sundays) and uses the voices of the cathedral choir. I almost wrote 'features' instead of 'uses' and there is a sense in which you are attending a concert rather than going to a service, which again might make a few regulars sniffy.

Whereas Larkin checked to see that his church was empty before he went in to indulge in essentially solitary reflection, my sense of church going is much more tied up with community. I love the feeling of being a part of something that has continued for centuries in the same building in largely the same way. Having rejected religion in my teenage years, I found myself coming back to it gradually and uncertainly. I wonder if anyone who has once been convinced of the intellectual arguments in favour of atheism can ever fully throw off his doubts and embrace religion wholeheartedly. I cannot argue anyone away from atheism and I would not try but I feel that they are missing something by refusing to go into churches or looking at them purely as museums.

Tourist guides go into church a lot and some of it obviously rubbed off onto me over the years. There has been no Pauline conversion so far - and I still find the Bible more beautiful than believable - but I am much less reluctant to think of myself as a church goer now.

TOURISM AND TERRORISM

Nervous travelers

A ll professions that are interesting tend to be overcrowded. There are always going to be more actors, writers and artists than the potential audience for their work justifies and the same is true in guiding, a smaller profession but one more subject to fluctuations in its fortunes. Artists, writers and performers can lobby the government and other sponsors for help but there will never be enough subsidy available to keep them all occupied. Guides do have times when they are very busy and operators and agencies are struggling to find people, but they also have to become used to periods of inactivity. These occur every year in the winter months, November to February, and in periods when business takes a sudden dip. There have been quite a few of those since 11th September 2001.

All guides and tour directors will be able to tell you where they were on what is now almost universally called 9/11. The use of the American abbreviation is important. While it is not exclusively a transatlantic industry, the number of Americans visiting the British Isles is an important barometer of prosperity in tourism and no discussion of the industry can avoid what happened on that day.

I had just finished supervising a group photograph in Killarney, a town in the west of Ireland that relies almost entirely on people coming to stay there before they drive around the scenic Ring of Kerry and then see the Killarney Lakes. It is a town devoted to tourism that consists of hotels, pubs and shops, and the homes of those who work in them. Con, our photographer, whispered to me conspiratorially about the attacks on the World Trade Centre while the group were returning to the coach or going on a jaunting cart ride with Billy Tangey and his crew of jovial locals. They would regale them with stories and songs for an hour before they checked in. In the evening we were due to go to an entertainment dinner where songs would be sung, more jokes told and people would feel they had seen a real piece of old Ireland. It is easy to mock this oirishness from the outside but the people who practice it are genuinely disarming and even jaundiced tour directors like myself become tied up with the jollity of it all.

Rarely can the contrast between fantasy and the reality have been so acute. I decided not to tell the people on the jaunting carts anything for the time being but said to the others that we had heard some bad news and would go to the hotel to find out more. Those who go on the ride with Billy and his crew always come back laughing and an hour later I had to bring them down with the news. It was impossible to avoid by that time and obviously affected the tone and content of the tour thereafter. This was not in a negative way. Many people expressed their satisfaction that, at a time of inexplicable chaos, they found some stability from being on a tour with sympathetic people. The fact of being in Ireland, with its strong American links, and the obviously genuine feelings of sympathy expressed towards the American people also helped.

There is a certain irony here. Ireland considers itself particularly close to the USA and many of those who tour there have Irish roots – or claim to have. It was once calculated that forty per cent of the USA's population claim Irish ancestry. The proportion claiming (or admitting to) roots in England is a fraction of that even though the actual number of emigrants from both countries is probably similar. What people remember is the headline figure of a million Irish leaving at the time of the potato famine in the middle of the nineteenth century and the fact that they maintained small intermarrying communities in the USA. They also remember the indifference and callousness of the British authorities towards Irish suffering at this time and the brutality of the suppression of Irish aspirations to freedom from British rule. Otherwise conservative and respectable members of their communities have a strange soft spot for the Irish freedom movements that are cousins to the pro-Palestinian suicide bombers who caused such damage to the fabric and self-respect of the USA.

While the Irish problem is inching towards a solution, largely as a result of the efforts of British and American intermediaries, particularly Bill Clinton, tourism in Northern Ireland is gradually opening up. In the nature of these things people are as much interested in the current manifestations as the historical origins of the tensions in Ireland. Guided tours are essentially visual experiences with explanations thrown in rather than intellectual theories demonstrated by visual means. The stark divisions between the unionist and republican communities can be seen on any tour of Belfast just by looking at the flags and wall paintings on display along the Ormeau and Shankhill Roads. What gives a little piquancy to these public demonstrations of loyalty to different causes is that the Irish republican neighbourhoods identify themselves with the oppressed Palestinians and display the emblems of the PLO next to their tricolours, while the unionists fly flags of the state of Israel to show where their inspiration comes from. Many Irish American tourists support the cause of Irish freedom and unification (which are the same thing to them) but have little time for the suicide bombers of Palestine who inspired those who attacked their own country. It is not so much a case of one man's freedom fighter being another man's terrorist, rather one century's dispossessed exiles becoming the next century's pillars of the establishment. The exiles took with them some of the values of their home country and preserved these in aspic for future generations. Meanwhile other alien and contradictory values grew up in the land they had left.

There is a further level of irony in the fact that many of the Irish emigrants to America were actually fiercely anti-

Catholic. They were descended from the Scots brought into Ulster in the sixteenth and seventeenth centuries to counter the power of the Catholic lords of Ireland whose loyalty was more to the Pope than to the crown. James I remarked that the Scots from his homeland were used enough to dancing through bogs and would therefore easily adjust to those of Ireland. These hard-working God-fearing people established themselves in what had been the most pugnaciously independent anti-British part of Ireland and there laid the foundations for the industrial successes of Northern Ireland, which have long since been overtaken by the republic in the south. Yet within a century they were streaming out of Ulster into emigrant ships that took them on the long, hard and dangerous journey to the USA.

Why did these successfully transplanted immigrants to Ireland leave for yet another new home across the Atlantic? Curiously, what should have been their greatest moment of triumph turned out to be the cause of their flight. On 12th July 1690 the Protestant King William of Orange defeated his Catholic father-in-law, the former King James II, at the battle of the Boyne. The date, of course, is still celebrated with notorious partisanship in parts of Northern Ireland, to such an extent that many Catholic families head south across the border to escape the gloating of their neighbours over an event that happened more than three centuries ago. A year after the battle, hostilities were still dragging on despite the fact that William had returned to London and James to France where he lived in embittered and increasingly pious exile. The fighting finally came to an end when the Catholic general Patrick Sarsfield surrendered to his Protestant counterpart Ginkel after being promised religious toleration for his people. Despite this promise of freedom the Protestant parliament in Dublin broke the agreement the two generals had made. (You can still see the Treaty Stone on which they signed the document next to the River Shannon in Limerick.) They passed a series of penal laws that were unashamedly designed to make the Catholics of Ireland permanent second-class citizens. These laws remained in place until 1829 when the British parliament gave at least theoretical equality to Catholics, largely as a result of the work of Daniel O'Connell, an Irish lawyer and campaigner for religious equality. O'Connell is now remembered in Ireland as 'the Liberator' and is commemorated in statues and street names throughout the republic.

In order to be even-handed in their discrimination the penal laws were also applied to the Ulster Presbyterians, despite the fact that they were the most virulently anti-Catholic inhabitants of Ireland. The laws were designed to support the Anglican church against all its rivals, Protestant non-conformist as well as Catholic. To this day this establishment is known as the Church of Ireland, which leads to a good deal of confusion for tourists. In a town of a thousand Catholics and a dozen Protestants (not uncommon in the southern part of the country) the older building with Church of Ireland on its notice board is kept going by the dozen while the newer churches are maintained by the thousand. The Ulster Presbyterians are not members of this church and, 300 years ago, they found that the fruits of their labours were to be used to support it as well as their own chapels, that the marriages which took place in their churches were not recognised and that they, like the Catholics, would not be able to own their own land.

As has happened on countless other occasions, a people confronted with a choice of giving up their faith or their homeland choose to remain loyal to their faith and find a new home. These were the Scots-Irish that many Americans claim descent from, the backbone of George Washington's army that fought for independence and the pioneers of expansion into the heart of the wild west. They were emphatically not the starving million Catholics who had no choice but to sail for America in the notorious 'coffin ships' that left Ireland during and after the potato famine in the mid nineteenth century. These later Irish exiles then congregated in towns and cities, formed the Irish American

166

communities of Chicago and Boston and celebrated their final acceptance into American emancipation when one of theirs, John F Kennedy, became the first Roman Catholic president of the USA in 1960. They also contributed money, knowingly or unknowingly, towards the IRA's terrorist campaigns against a British presence in Northern Ireland. Very few of them gave support to the PLO, despite the identification between the two organisations.

These contradictions were a long way from our minds as we watched the television images of planes flying into buildings. In fact many guides will have had contradictory feelings of their own. If they are honest most of them will admit that their first thoughts, after the scale of the devastation sank in, were of how the events would affect their income. The gap between the concern and the calculation was probably short enough to be insignificant in many cases.   This is hardly surprising or particularly shameful. Everyone will look at major events of this nature from a wide and from a narrow perspective. It does not show a lack of sympathy with the victims if you are simultaneously concerned about the effect their deaths will have on your livelihood. We can hold the outrage, horror and sympathy at the same time as we worry whether we will be able to afford the mortgage next year.

Although it was not in the thoughts of the hijackers, the timing of their attacks could not have been worse from the point of view of guides. Incoming tourism had just been recovering from a poor season caused by, of all things, the foot and mouth outbreak. It is worth looking at the sequence of events to show just how vulnerable a feel-good industry like tourism can be to events beyond its control. A farmer buys in contaminated food for his pigs, neglects basic hygiene precautions and starts an outbreak of the disease his colleagues fear above all others. A system of farming subsidy that encourages the movement of livestock causes it to spread rapidly. The government, under pressure from farming interests, begins a programme of mass slaughter to combat it. The carcasses of healthy animals sent to their deaths are burned in open fields, their legs grotesquely sticking up in the air through the smoke. Television cameras film the process and their pictures are broadcast around the world. Thousands of people in the USA, thinking about a holiday in Britain but with thoughts of mad cow disease at the back of their minds, see the pictures and decide to go to Hawaii instead. Hundreds of tourist guides face starvation, ruin and personal tragedy. (Alright, that last bit is slightly exaggerated.) Trace the line back far enough and you can probably find a butterfly flapping its wings somewhere on the other side of the world. The end result is the same – a group of disgruntled guides waiting for the phone to ring.

Again it may seem callous to moan about our fate when farmers face ruin through the carelessness of one of their colleagues and the lethargy or incompetence of official bodies. But it is hardly unnatural. In guiding you do not earn if you do not work. Even most of those with fairly steady jobs working for the same company all the time will be paid on a purely daily basis. There is no sick pay or paid holidays and no-one can expect redundancy if the work dries up. You simply receive a letter regretting that your services will not be required for the coming season. Sometimes notice that your services are no longer required comes in the form of silence, the telephone that refuses to ring. Companies themselves are subject to these same fluctuations and may go out of business suddenly when a downturn occurs or the owner decides to retire or move on.

If the foot and mouth downturn was a frustrating, almost farcical, problem for tourism, it was also a temporary one. The problems caused by the suicide attacks at the end of that year were of an altogether different nature. In the short term people were not able to get onto an aeroplane to come to Britain. In the longer term, they were less willing to do so. This was not a new problem but the culmination of something which had begun sixteen years earlier in 1985 when gunmen had attacked airports throughout Europe that

CHAPTER TWELVE

were full of American tourists in a random and brutal retaliation for their country's perceived support of Israel.

   With what now seems idiotically bad timing and lack of foresight I had given up a relatively secure position with one company and gone on a winter trip to the Middle East, intending to launch myself on the freelance market when I returned in the spring. My excuse now is that tourism had never felt threatened by terrorism before these airport attacks and the downturn in business took most of us by surprise. In fact, we were becoming complacent about terrorism, having been subjected to the IRA's intermittent bombing campaigns. A bomb had gone off in the Tower of London and killed several people but this did not close either the attraction or the industry. A bag search was introduced for everyone going into the Tower and business went back to normal. There were a few delays caused by the searches and, as is the nature of such stable door exercises, nothing suspicious has been found since.
   After a while the IRA gave up bombing London and then gave up bombing altogether and took up negotiation. While the bombing continued it was more of a threat to visitors to Britain than suicide attacks would ever be. Yet the first had a very slight effect on business, while the second had a huge impact. There are two reasons for this, the first to do with the motivation, the second with method.
   The IRA bombing campaigns occurred mainly in the seventies and early eighties when business was booming. Strike-bound, depressed and cheap, the pre and early Thatcher Britain of the late seventies and early eighties was ideal for American tourists, quite happy to see their capitalism working better than our socialism. People tend to visit countries that are similar to but poorer than their own. This not only makes them feel richer, but also a little smug. Visiting countries with more successful economies leads to feelings of inferiority and envy which are compounded by the seemingly outrageous cost of a cup of coffee or glass of

beer. So we go to Spain rather than Germany or Japan and the Americans come to Britain. The Queen's Silver Jubilee celebrations in the wet summer of 1977 brought huge numbers of tourists and they continued to come through the early and mid eighties when the pound was very low against not only the dollar of the USA but that of Canada, Australia and New Zealand.

This came to an end abruptly in 1986. Air travel had been largely unaffected by terrorism at that time. True, some planes were hijacked but they were not used as weapons by their hijackers, more as a means of making a point or an escape. As security on aeroplanes was increased, passengers at airports were targeted. This led to the attacks in 1985 when random bullets were fired in the direction of innocent American tourists checking in for their flights home. For the first time being a terrorist target was not a case of being in the wrong place at the wrong time but of being the wrong nationality.

Talking to people from the USA in the late eighties guides in Britain were struck by how personally threatened tourists felt by these attacks. Years of IRA attacks had made us feel that terrorism was both idiotically random and statistically insignificant as far as our own safety was concerned. We would put up with bag and even body searches if necessary but the chance of a Londoner being hit by a bomb planted by an Irishman were considerably less than those of being hit by a car driven by an Englishman and neither was big enough to make us cancel our days and evenings out in the centre of London or to give in to the people who were trying to make our lives a misery.

In the USA they had not built up this kind of bravado. America had not been attacked since Pearl Harbour in 1941, and the experience of being the target of terrorism was unwelcomely new to them. Few of them felt any inclination to increase the statistical chances of being victims, no matter how unlikely these were. Lots of comments were made about this apparent timidity from a people who were otherwise very lax about the control of personal weaponry. Statistics showed how much more danger was posed by a Saturday night special than by a Kalashnikov, that they were in more danger of dying in the bath than being killed by a terrorist. But it is the new danger that attracts attention not the old one. Deaths in the bath and by Saturday nighters were a part of life in the States; terror attacks targeted specifically at them were not. The IRA were setting off bombs meant for the British and could be largely ignored, while the pro-Palestinian Moslems were specifically targeting Americans and could not.

Moreover, they were targeting them at the place where they felt most vulnerable – in the air. One of the most feared ways of dying is surely in an air crash. Car accidents hold relatively little fear despite being far more common. Otherwise calm and rational people go into cold sweats on entering an aeroplane, all statistics about their relative safety soon forgotten as the roar of the engine prepares to take that huge metal bullet into the air. The combination of height, speed and helplessness are what terrifies us. There is something intimate and dangerously beguiling about a motor car that convinces you that you are in control and that you are near enough to the ground not to feel threatened if anything goes wrong. None of this exists on a plane, designed to fly above the clouds at far greater speeds and in an enclosed space with it own atmosphere totally separated from the surrounding environment.

Most of us imagine what it would be like in the moments before a crash when it is obvious you are going to die but before you actually do so. This is a relatively brief period in a car accident and death is by no means certain. It could be much longer in an air accident and the chances of escape are insignificant. No safety precautions or skill at the controls will help the air passenger on a doomed plane, while the car passenger or driver might be lucky. These terrible last moments are probably what make the families of air crash victims so distraught at their loss, the feeling that their son or daughter knew what was going to happen but could do nothing about it.

The families of those who died in the Lockerbie air crash in 1988 had to deal with these feelings as well as the knowledge that the Pan Am flight carrying their loved ones was sabotaged. The so-called Lockerbie bombers had almost certainly never heard of the little town in Scotland that gave them that name when they planted their bomb. The plane they targeted left Heathrow twenty minutes late and, without this delay, would have probably exploded above the Atlantic, sparing the people of Lockerbie a dozen lives and the town its unwanted fame.

There was a terrible progressive logic about the way air terrorism developed. First the planes were hijacked in remote places and taken off route but usually returned with their crews and passengers. Then passengers were targeted at overseas airports before they could board their planes. Next a plane heading home was blown up remotely in the air with no warning or hope for those on board. Finally planes were commandeered and turned into weapons for use against people on the ground. Each strike was designed to drive deeper into the heart of the fears of the people being targeted. No wonder the average American was becoming more and more reluctant to enter an aeroplane and head in the direction of where the trouble was coming from.

It is no use arguing logically against these fears, pointing out that Britain is a long way from the Middle East and that the statistical chances of being attacked by terrorists are so remote as to be insignificant. Tourism is such a feel-good industry that even raising the subject of security is enough to make people change their minds about travelling. When the number of tourists coming to Britain dipped sharply in 1986 in the aftermath of the terrorist attacks on European airports, the government, worried about the effect on the economy, made the mistake of starting a campaign of reassurance to attract American visitors back. Pictures appeared on television of armed police at Heathrow airport ready to protect the few people who arriving there.

With hindsight this was a mistake. Britain is supposed to be the country of *unarmed* policemen with their curious tall hats and smiling faces who will tell you which bus to get to your hotel and wish you good day, ma'am. Flak jackets and machine guns are not part of the image of the British bobby. Instead of reassuring people, this seemed to be telling them they would be entering a war zone: a safe war zone, but a war zone all the same. Likewise, telling them that human beings cannot catch foot and mouth disease so they have nothing to fear in seeing the British countryside undermines the whole point of a vacation in the UK. Want to see burning carcasses on holiday? Come over here – we've got plenty. No thanks, we prefer lambs gambolling in the fields.

Is there anything that can be done to counter the negative images that tend to accompany safety campaigns? Realistically, the only thing to be done is to stay calm and to wait. You cannot argue people out of essentially irrational fears. The Mayor of Toronto, when his city was put off-limits by the World Health Authority because of an outbreak of Sars, told anyone who would listen that Sars was not a problem in his city, that it was quite safe to visit and that the WHA was out of order. So stridently did he say this that his outbursts almost certainly had the opposite effect to what he intended and drew even more attention to a problem that would pass sooner or later. A resigned shrug and a low profile often achieve more than a strident denial. To quote a phrase, he would say that wouldn't he?

How long does a place have to wait until people feel safe to travel there again? A year is the generally accepted length of time before memories fade, but some people need longer and some less. Tourists are not a homogenous group. While most tend to take the safe option, some people are positively attracted to trouble spots. Israel, whose once thriving tourist industry is now in ruins, has found that some people are travelling there to see how they fight the threat of terror and to learn about life in a war zone. They are a fairly dedicated minority, however. Most people simply turn the page of their brochure to find a less threatening destination, until next year at least.

Not only do negative perceptions fade after a year or so, but people will become used to the demands of security. They may gradually develop the kind of attitude that most British did in response to the IRA campaigns – a mixture of resignation, irritation and a kind of stubborn defiance, a refusal to be bamboozled into acting the way terrorists want us to. Even if we do concede that they may have a point, we do not want to be seen to give in to them.

A parallel is with the way that motor car manufacturers sold car safety. When Ford introduced it into its advertising in the USA in the early 1960s their sales dipped so alarmingly that they soon abandoned their campaign strategy of showing slow motion films of test cars being crashed in order to demonstrate how safe their vehicles were. Ford was selling safety that year, while General Motors and Chrysler were selling cars, went the industry maxim. Yet, today safety is an essential feature of car advertising and a little sub genre has developed in which creatives spend time and money thinking up ways of showing cars crashing in spectacular and funny ways. Nobody turns away in disgust from this anymore. They have accepted that safety is a part of advertising now and join in the joke or admire the spectacle.

In the same way September 11th may have a curiously beneficial effect on tourism in the long term. A people previously immune from terrorism suddenly find that it has struck right into the heart of their country. They have to join the rest of the world now and build the experience of being attacked into their everyday lives. This might make them more rather than less willing to travel in the long term as they develop the kind of sang sang-froid the British liked to feel they showed in the face of the IRA. Security checks and armed police are taken for granted as part of the business of travel.

They will also become more discriminating about which countries they travel to, rather than just lumping everything across the Atlantic as possibly dangerous. While the intifada and its consequences have virtually destroyed mainstream tourism in Israel, there are signs that potential tourists realise that there is over a thousand miles between London and Jerusalem, that one is almost always safe while the other is potentially explosive.

This may be one of the reasons why the British government almost always supports the American administration in its determination to punish what it sees as dangerous regimes by military force. It would be fanciful to say that Blair was backing Bush's attack on Iraq just in order to boost domestic tourism, but there is a sense in which politics and travel are linked. Americans coming to Britain do so with a sense of confidence often lacking in their visits to Europe. Not only is the language the same but there is a belief that our wars against each other were concluded two hundred years ago and that we are on the same side now.

This came home to me as I was conducting a tour of London and we passed 10 Downing Street on the way up Whitehall. Tony Blair had recently become Prime Minister and I mentioned the fact, aware that some of the group might not be familiar with him yet. Somewhat to my surprise they all were and an elderly man even said out loud, "I like him" to general murmurs of approval. A Labour politician liked and admired by an elderly American tourist? I was flabbergasted. That was the time when I realised that socialism was dead, in Britain at least.

It was entirely possible that the gentleman who so admired Tony Blair was not even aware that he was leader of a party that had once claimed to be socialist. To him the Prime Minister was a clean cut articulate family man with Christian values, the sort of person who could be a popular young politician in the USA with little difficulty. He has, moreover, the quality which successful British politicians need to be taken seriously in the USA. He is reassuring without being servile and he does not seem to have an anti-American instinct in his body, unlike some of his predecessors (or his colleagues). Winston Churchill, still universally admired in the USA, had this quality, as did Margaret Thatcher. Neil Kinnock did not and neither did Eden nor John Major.

Tourist guides need this quality just as much as politicians. There is a distinction between working in the service industry and being servile, one which we are not always clear about in Britain. Successful tour companies often devote a page or more of their brochures to extolling the virtues and talents of their staff. Their qualifications might not be mentioned, but they are praised for being knowledgeable, informative, multi-lingual, good-humoured and helpful. Most of all, they say, these people are your friends. They are dedicated to looking after you in a new environment. People need to feel that degree of confidence in the people they are travelling with as well as the countries they are travelling to when they purchase their tickets. Without it, they will not even get on the plane.

CHAPTER THIRTEEN:

LOSING OUR MARBLES

Museum guiding and the Parthenon Marbles

When I started guiding it seemed natural to name the sculptures from the Parthenon after the man who brought them to Britain rather than the place they came from. Lord Elgin, we were told, had saved the Marbles from almost certain destruction by bringing them to Britain and had spent £75,000 of his own money in doing so. The £35,000 which the British government had given him in return seemed a paltry reward for an altruistic Europhile who had put conservation before profit. As a small compensation at least his name would be remembered when people looked at these beautiful carvings.

And they are exceptionally beautiful. They represent the Athens of Pericles four and a half centuries before Christ, the city that defied the might of the Persian empire and united the Greeks against her bullying neighbour. In particular they show the procession that took place every four years of the citizens of the city to the Athenaeum, the temple of Athene, when the goddess was presented with a woollen robe or peplops by the grateful people. The robe can be seen in the section opposite the entrance to the Duveen gallery and around it sit the gods, identifiable by signs such as the hat and cloak of Hermes (better known by his Roman name of Mercury) and the crutch of Athene's brother Hephaistos. The skill of the carvers led by the great Phidias can be clearly seen, although the carvings themselves have been worn and damaged by centuries of neglect, vandalism and warfare. Elgin, we were taught, was the hero of the hour who had prevented their total destruction and had saved them for civilisation.

It therefore came as something of a surprise when, as a newly qualified guide, I took a mixed nationality group on a tour of London and mentioned the museum and its marbles as we passed through Bloomsbury, only for a Greek member of the party to call out, "Ah, those are the ones you stole!" His compatriots laughed at this and, as I explained Lord Elgin's good intentions, I realised I had already lost the initiative. I felt like one of those people who insisted we should celebrate the millennium at the beginning of 2001 – technically correct maybe, but somewhat late for the party.

I have long since learned to get my retaliation in first. If I have anybody of Greek origin (or sympathy) when going by the British Museum these days, I tell them that it is one of the great treasure houses of international culture but not very well named because the exhibits come from all over the world, not just Britain. They are welcome to see them for free but – slight pause while I look at the potential Marble returner – they cannot take them away when they leave.

One of the golden rules of guiding is that you never win an argument with a tourist – so there is no point in getting into one. Even if you know you are in the right and your client admits as much, they will resent you for getting one over them and this will affect the way they treat you at the end of the tour when they decide whether to tip or have a questionnaire to fill in. The best thing is to agree to disagree and make as light of it as you can. This is why it is a good idea to avoid politics except in the most general and non-partisan way.

That does not mean you should always shy away from discussion or potential controversy. Nowadays I often bring up the subject of the marbles and the best place for them to live and ask people for their views. Opinion is divided and debate is usually friendly but I feel that the majority of people are becoming sympathetic to the idea of returning them to Athens - although they are always glad that to have seen them in London. Like most great works of art they have an accessibility that appeals to teenagers and professors alike. Anyone can appreciate the skill with which the carvers represent the impatient young horsemen in the procession being forced to rear their mounts as the weight of numbers makes the line move slowly. People also like to hear stories of the impetuous and argumentative Greek gods, the original dysfunctional family.

I used to start a tour of the British Museum at the Marbles and end in the library next to the Magna Carta, partly so that we could finish on a British note and partly so that people could then look at the other manuscripts on display there. These included the Lindisfarne Gospels, an illustrated manuscript of the Bible and manuscript versions of musical works by composers such as Handel and, the one that most people headed for, the Beatles. These documents, however, have been moved a mile away to the British Library's own building at St Pancras and so I now end at the Marbles and this gives people a chance to enjoy them on their own and then wander over to the new Great Court and patronise the gift shop. The British Museum is still free but it needs all the business it can get.

A guiding friend says that it is the Marbles that keep the museum free of charge. In the game of moral one-upmanship that has developed around the Marbles the fact that five million people a year can see these works without paying for them gives us enough of an edge over the Greeks to resist demands for their return. This campaign was headed for many years by the late Melina Mercouri, Greek actress and Minister of Culture, who refused even to utter Elgin's name and identified him as a despoiler, robber and imperialist, the chief villain of the story.

This seems a bit harsh on Thomas Bruce, the seventh Earl of Elgin, who was ambassador in Greece when he saw the condition of the marbles and began the expensive process of bringing them to Britain. The £75,000 which he claims to have spent on this task is Elgin's own figure and includes a little creative accountancy, such as interest payments and bribes, for which one can hardly expect reliable receipts. Nevertheless, the £35,000 he was given by parliament in return fell well short of his outgoings. If he was a robber, he was not a very good one. What sort of thief loses twice as much as he makes in his biggest heist?

On closer examination, Elgin does not appear either the saint we have sometimes made him out to be or the villain that Ms Mercouri painted him as. He suffered from syphilis, which is probably why he wanted the post in Greece, as his doctors had advised him to live in a warm climate. His sexual life is only a half-open book, but it seems to have been quite active. He divorced his first wife and then remarried, fathering eleven children in all. The expenses of supporting this large offspring exhausted his funds and those of the first countess and money was a pressing problem by the time he came to dispose of the marbles. The wars with Napoleon's France, which had much to do with the growth of the Museum in the early nineteenth century, led to him being detained there as he tried to make his way back from Greece.

What sticks in the throat of the Greeks – and what I did not fully realise until I read it in the British Museum's own book on the marbles – is that Elgin was not ambassador to Greece but to the Ottoman Empire. These were the equivalents of the bullying Persians that Pericles and his fellow citizens had successfully defied over twenty centuries earlier. The Turks were delighted that Lord Nelson had defeated Napoleon in Egypt and were only too happy to release the marbles to this eccentric British aristocrat. The subject peoples of Greece were given no say in the matter as the marbles were somewhat unskilfully brought to the ground, packed up and shipped away from the Acropolis to Bloomsbury.

Elgin's original plan had been to take casts of the marbles and then recreate them back in Britain but a combination of the evangelical enthusiasm of his advisor and chaplain Philip Hunt, the rapidly deteriorating condition of the marbles and Turkish (not Greek) indifference led the copying operation to turn into a large removal exercise. What you see in the Duveen room represents under half the original marbles and about two thirds of what was there when Elgin first saw them in 1799.

Two incidents, one well known and one not, illustrate the neglect and vandalism that affected the Parthenon and hurried Elgin into his act of rescue (or theft). In 1687 the Parthenon, having been the temple of Athene, a church and a mosque, had been reduced to the indignity of use as an arsenal. A large store of gunpowder was ignited by a shell from the besieging Venetian forces and the subsequent explosion was the single most devastating piece of damage to this wonder of ancient architecture. (If you wish to see it as it was before the explosion there is a small model in a side gallery next to the Duveen room - or a full size version made from concrete in Nashville, Tennessee.) A smaller example of neglect comes from the story that Elgin purchased a house on the Acropolis in the hope of finding further carvings buried under the ground. The Turkish owner pocketed the money before cheerfully admitting that he had already destroyed the statues and used the marble from them in building the house.

In the end it is pointless judging people of one century by the standards of another. In the face of the combination of neglect and vandalism that Elgin and his crew found, it is no wonder they were not over-concerned with the niceties of legal propriety and just wanted to save what they could. Not surprisingly, given the history of the site, they felt that they could do a better job of this in Britain than in Greece. Yet we should not be too sniffy about how other countries neglect their ancient monuments. Just take a look at Hadrian's Wall or Stonehenge if you want to see neglected treasures.

Perceptions change as time passes and actions that can be seen as altruistic in one century appear insensitive in another. This is reflected in shifts of language. Just as hardly anybody now uses the words 'negro' or 'coloured' to describe someone who is black, few people call these carvings the Elgin Marbles today (although the British Museum itself still uses that name on the front of its very useful book on them). Melina Mercouri, although she never lived to see them returned to Athens, did at least persuade us to use the more neutral term Parthenon Marbles, or Sculptures from the Parthenon. The dream of returning them to Athens for the Olympics is no longer viable, although the Greek authorities claim to have plans for a building to house them when the British government/people/Museum see the light.

There is a momentum in the marbles campaign that seems to be gathering steam slowly but inexorably. The British Museum argues that it would take an Act or Parliament to return the Marbles to Greece as they were given by an Act originally when Elgin was offered the take it or leave it sum of £35,000. If, moreover, the marbles were returned this would represent our old friend thin end of wedge. The Egyptians have made noises about the Rosetta Stone, which only came to Britain because Nelson defeated the French at the Battle of the Nile. (There is nothing like a successful military campaign to boost a country's cultural stockpiles.) African countries have demanded the return of dubiously acquired treasures in tandem with compensation for the historic evil of slavery and even the Geordies in the north east of England want the return of the Lindisfarne Gospels - a nice parochial version of the marbles dispute that is now the concern of the new British Library.

Take this process to its logical conclusion and, not only would the British Museum itself cease to exist, but all works of art would have to return to their homelands. No artist would be able to sell a work abroad as buyers feared forced requisition without compensation. Eventually people in Britain would only be able to see British art, Italians would only see Italian art and Finns Finnish art. This might be alright if you were Italian, tolerable if you were British but a bit tough on the Finns. In any case, it is against what both art and tourism are about, which is exploring and celebrating the cultures of different countries. I enjoy seeing a Constable or a Turner painting but it is the feeling of familiarity that pleases me. I can learn more from seeing the sculptures and paintings of another country and another era.

An example of how this cross pollination of cultures works in an interesting way can be found almost directly above the marbles on the first floor of the British Museum. The Portland Vase is my favourite piece in the Museum and I always spend a few minutes there when I take groups through. Again the name comes from the British aristocrat who donated it, although in this case he was not also the one to discover it. It was found by William Hamilton, another ambassador, this time to the Court of the King of Naples, and husband of Emma, who was herself the lover of Lord Nelson. (Hamilton was almost certainly aware of this affair and turned a blind eye to it.) Both Nelson and Hamilton had peripheral roles in the acquisition of the Parthenon/Elgin Marbles but the vase was a much smaller item, acquired and disposed of legally as part of the genteel looting of the Mediterranean countries that took place as British military and economic power increased.

The Portland Vase came originally from Italy but little is known about it and much guesswork is involved in interpreting the figures carved in the upper layer of white glass which sits on top of the blue layer beneath. The accepted wisdom is that the carving shows the wedding of Peleus and Thetis. Peleus the man wooed and won the goddess Thetis and their child was Achilles, who was dipped in the mythical River Styx by his mother to give him extraordinary powers in battle. He grew up to become the greatest and proudest of Greek warriors but his weakness was in the heel by which his mother had gripped him during his immersion in the magic river. Teenagers who have no knowledge of mythology and are more interested in sport will still have heard of the Achilles tendon which is next to the ankle and can relate to this story.

The Portland Vase was originally thought to be pointed at the bottom but at some stage in its life this was replaced by a flat circular piece of blue and white glass which can now be seen next to the vase itself. This is thought to represent the Judgement of Paris and the figure represented certainly seems to be in the process of making his mind up. He, the most handsome man in the world, had to choose the most beautiful of the three goddesses – Hera, Athene or Aphrodite. He chose Aphrodite, better known as Venus, who had offered him the bribe of the world's most beautiful woman. This was Helen of Troy and it was her elopement with Paris that led to the ten year Trojan War and the eventual defeat of Troy by means of the Trojan horse (another well-known reference). This fulfilled the ancient prophecy that Paris would bring about the fall of his home city. It was during this war that the great Achilles was eventually killed by an arrow fired by Paris that hit him in his only vulnerable spot – his Achilles heel.

Soon after the vase was purchased by Portland it was put on display in the Museum while still under his ownership but smashed into pieces by a mad Irishman called William Lloyd. Why he did so is not known but he had come from a respectable family and then developed a drink problem. Because of law at the time and the fact that the Vase was still owned by Portland and not the museum, the only punishment available to the magistrates was to fine Lloyd five pounds or to imprison him for two weeks. He had no money but one of his family paid the fine for him and he then disappeared into the mists of history. Meanwhile the museum staff lovingly and carefully put the toothpaste back into the tube by pasting the pieces back together. Josiah Wedgwood, the Staffordshire potter, then began work on making a copy of the vase. After much painstaking work he eventually succeeded and the statue of him at the Wedgwood Centre in Barlaston near Stoke shows Josiah holding his version of the vase. This inspired the white on blue style known as Jasperware, one that the Wedgwood company is still famous for.

A few minutes at the Portland Vase, a small work about a foot high and a quarter of an inch think, can touch on ancient mythology, the skills of the Italian glassmakers, sport and the human body, the vagaries of the legal system, the skill of the museum staff, a sex scandal two hundred years ago and shopping, that mainstay of modern tourism. There should be something for everybody there.

A lot of guiding involves this kind of cross-referencing of cultures, marrying things that people have heard of with what is new. I am reminded of Samuel Johnson's remark that the job of the poet is to make the new familiar and the familiar new. Many guides are only involved with showing aspects of their own country to people from overseas but sometimes you can have fun jumping around different time zones and geographical areas. One guide I know does a very interesting tour of Westminster Abbey for Americans simply by pointing out all the places in the USA that have connections with the Abbey. You can overdo this – it is worth making the new familiar as well as the familiar new – but linking parts of the tour to what is well known is a good way to keep peoples' attention.

The British Museum has plenty of opportunity for developing this kind of guiding skill. It is not a place I guide in often but I enjoy going back to prepare tours of it. You have between one and two hours to cover all the major works in the collection and, inevitably, there will omissions in a highlights tour. The main stops will be the Reading Room of the library, the Egyptian mummies, Portland Vase, Rosetta Stone, and the reliefs from the Assyrian Place of Ashurbanipal and a few genuinely British finds like the recently excavated Lindow Man and the Sutton Hoo treasure. I also like to show people the beautiful statue of Demeter searching for her daughter Persephone in the underworld and the few parts of the Mausoleum of Halicarnasus that were saved and brought to Bloomsbury.

Saved or stolen? The debate is academic but also urgent. There is no undoing the actions of Lord Elgin and the other cultural entrepreneurs of his day two centuries ago but there is an opportunity to address the grievances felt by the Greeks. Elgin's work was continued by Lord Duveen with what the Greeks see as a similar lack of sensitivity. Duveen was a successful and very wealthy art dealer of the interwar years who in 1939 donated funds for the gallery where the marbles are now displayed. This is a spacious and attractive room designed in the same dimensions as the Parthenon, but to show the marbles facing inwards and at an easily seen height, rather than outwards at the top of the columns which would have kept them largely hidden from the eyes of all but the goddess in the original temple. Duveen, however, marred his philanthropy somewhat by insisting that the marbles should be cleaned before being displayed. Workmen were assigned to brush and polish the marbles with more vigour than expertise until they achieved a pristine brightness.

This buffing up of the marbles is still subject to great criticism, particularly from the marble returners looking for a self-righteous stick to hit the museum with. Such is often the case when works of art are cleaned and restored. Again, there is limited value in condemning the people of one generation for following fashions that have since changed. Whatever the merits of his vigorous cleaning process, it would be a shame to waste Duveen's fine space if the marbles were sent back to Greece, where a new building would house them.

However, why not return to Elgin's original intention, which was to make casts of the carvings so as to preserve them? We have technologies undreamt of by Elgin or even Duveen and computer scanning equipment allied to the kind of skills first developed in restoring the Portland Vase could surely give us perfect copies of the marbles which could then be displayed in the Duveen Gallery. (If the job could be done in secret I doubt if one in a hundred people looking at them would even notice.) The originals could go to Greece, on long term loan if a transfer of ownership proved too difficult to arrange, and the British would once again feel that they were doing the decent thing, which has always been important to us as a nation.

Certain conditions would need to be attached to the

transfer of the marbles to Greece. These would basically involve saying 'please' and 'thank you'. At the moment British people going to Athens are almost invariably given a lecture on their countryman's nefarious acts, but they would have to acknowledge that his actions did much to rescue these works for posterity, even if they were insensitive by today's standards. A form of words could be agreed for the display areas in the new museum and his much-maligned reputation could be restored. British experience in looking after the marbles could also be used to ensure that the new space they were displayed in offered sufficient protection.

Of course, Greek pride might refuse to agree to terms such as these. Alternatively they might agree and, once they had the marbles back, could break an agreement they said was forced on them and continue to denigrate Elgin, Duveen and other arrogant Britons. This would, however, lose them the moral high ground, which they have gradually been ascending. A big signing ceremony that acknowledged but buried past differences on both sides would be enough for us to clamber back up the slope we have gradually been slipping down.

The British people gave up their empire because they were ultimately embarrassed into doing so by people like Gandhi: he made us feel uncomfortable because we were seen (and began to see ourselves) as oppressors and bullies. The same process will probably lead to us giving up the marbles eventually. Neil McGregor, the head of the British Museum, is a humane and liberal man who cannot feel easy that his institution is being identified with the kind of imperial arrogance of the Victorians. Surely it is better to act magnanimously rather than to fight a losing rearguard action.

Duplicating and then surrendering the Parthenon Sculptures would also have the effect of undermining the absurd obsession with both originality and ownership that makes the art world value a painting at over ten million pounds and a decent copy of it at less than five pounds.

While a painting has certain features that might not

come out through careful reproduction a sculpture or carving has none. A tour of the museum could still climax at the Duveen Gallery. The knowledge that you were not showing the original carvings of Pheidias and his crew would be tempered by the feeling that you could demonstrate British good grace and magnanimity.

Perfect replicas displayed in Bloomsbury, the originals back at the Acropolis, Greek pride assuaged, British magnanimity re-established and the reputation of Lord Elgin rehabilitated: is all this possible or just a pipe dream? I am sure that this is the course that Lord Elgin, looking down from his connoisseur's lodge in heaven, would approve of if his name was restored and the marbles returned home. He was probably sick of them by the time they had been offloaded in any case.

And I would finally have found an answer for that Greek tourist in my party – twenty years too late.

CHAPTER FOURTEEN:
THE POWER OF A POEM
Using literature

O n my very first extended tour of Britain, I suddenly found myself travelling towards the West Country with nothing to say. Nowadays I would just let people sleep until kicking into the story of Francis Drake, the Spanish Armada and that game of bowls he is supposed to have played while Philip of Spain's ships sailed past. At the time, however, as a qualified guide I felt it necessary to provide some form of commentary, so I recited a poem. It was Browning's Home Thoughts from Abroad:

> *O, to be in England, now that April's there*
> *And whoever wakes in England*
> *Sees, some morning, unaware*
> *That the lowest boughs and the brushwood*
> * sheaf*
> *Round the elm-tree bole are in tiny leaf,*
> *While the chaffinch sings on the orchard*
> * bough*
> *In England – now!*
>
> *And after April, when May follows,*
> * The whitethroat builds, and all the*
> * swallows!*
> * Hark, where my blossomed pear tree in the*
> * hedge*
> * Leans to the field and scatters on the clover*
> *Blossoms and dewdrops – at the bent*
> * spray's edge*
> *That's the wise thrush; he sings each song*
> * twice over,*
> *Lest you think he never could recapture*

The first fine careless rapture!
And though the fields seem rough with
* hoary dew,*
All will be gay when noontide wakes anew
The buttercups, the little children's dower
Far brighter than this gaudy melon flower!

The poem had nothing to do with the area we were in, but it was at that time of year when spring was turning to summer, so it seemed appropriate. The group seemed to enjoy it and even gave a little clap. It began a habit I developed of throwing in a poem or a reading every so often. I probably have enough poems committed to memory now to do one every day over a two week tour, but this might be overdoing it, so I ration them these days.

Not everybody likes the poems – there are probably plenty of people who consider me an over-educated idiot – but enough people do to make it worthwhile. It just seems silly to go to Stratford without hearing at least a little bit of Shakespeare, to Scotland without tackling the language and thoughts of Robert Burns, or to the Lake District without Wordsworth. These people, after all, are one of the reasons people come to Britain, inspired by the stories and poems of our greatest writers.

One of the reasons I use poetry is because if is a way of expressing patriotism. Now patriotism is not the most fashionable virtue these days. It smacks of jingoism and unthinking loyalty. People who are not afraid to say that they love their spouses, partners or children become embarrassed at the thought of saying they love their country. Yet we should surely love our country in the same way that we love our children – with total commitment but under no illusions. You do not have to think that your children are the most talented and best behaved in the world to care for them, just as you do not start watching a World Cup by selecting the most skilful team to support. You support your own, enjoying their

CHAPTER FOURTEEN

triumphs and suffering their failures.

William Blake expressed something of this in his famous poem Jerusalem, the first half of which is simply a series of questions. While he had only a handful of admirers in his lifetime, Blake's work lives on in a curious way, one that he could never have predicted and may not even have approved of. Blake was a rebel, an outsider, a strange visionary who lived an intense spiritual life but found the real world hard to come to terms with. He argued with most of his friends and only his devoted wife remained loyal to him as he tried to scrape a living through poetry, painting and engraving. How odd that this prickly rebel should write a poem that has become the battle hymn of the English establishment:

And did those feet in ancient time
Walk upon England's mountains green?
And was the holy lamb of God
On England's pleasant pastures seen?

And did that Countenance Divine
Shine forth upon these clouded hills?
And was Jerusalem builded here
Among these dark, satanic mills?

Bring me my bow of burning gold!
Bring me my arrow of desire!
Bring me my shield! O clouds unfold!
Bring me my chariots of fire!

I will not cease from mental fight
Nor shall my sword sleep in my hand,
Till we have built Jerusalem
In England's green and pleasant land.

There are plenty of evocative lines here. (Even the passenger with no interest in poems recognises the film titles.) The two famous lines, which contrast with each other, are at the end of the second and final verses. Blake lived in the world of dark satanic mills at the height of the industrial revolution and he seems to have been far more at home amongst them than the green and pleasant England of his imagination. The poem wonders aloud whether the boy Christ had come here carried on the back of his mother's uncle, Joseph of Arimithea. It is, frankly, a nonsensical idea. There is virtually no chance that a young boy could have travelled that distance, even with a wealthy trader who later turned missionary, as his guide. Blake, however, despised concepts such as geography. He lived a spirit life and, if he imagined that something happened, then that was a kind of reality for him. He had a very practical side, however, and, having trained as an engraver, he illustrated his own and other's poems with a method he devised himself.

Blake's Jerusalem is part of a larger work on Milton, the man who was alternately hero and villain to him. It was set to music by Parry in 1916 when, exhausted by a long war, the country needed an uplifting anthem. Since then it has become a kind of unofficial national anthem for England and the song of the Women's Institute. It will be familiar to many tourists from the film Calendar Girls.

Blake's Jerusalem fits into a visit to Glastonbury where King Arthur was reputedly buried and where Joseph is supposed to have buried the Holy Grail that Arthur's knights went in search of. Browning's Home Thoughts was written in Italy where he eloped with Elizabeth Barrett and is, therefore, not tied to any one place in England. Browning was very much the London gentleman and is buried in Poet's Corner at Westminster Abbey, while Elizabeth lies in the Protestant Cemetery in Florence. Another great patriotic English poem works best on a visit to Cambridge where Rupert Brooke spent much of his life. His poem The Soldier is, like Browning's, written as he remembers the beauties of his home country when he travels abroad, in this case never to return:

If I should die, think only this of me:
That there's some corner of a foreign field
That is forever England. There shall be
In that rich earth a richer dust concealed;
A dust whom England bore, shaped, made aware
Gave once her flowers to love, her ways to roam
A body of England, breathing English air,
Washed by the rivers, blessed by suns of home
And think this heart, all evil shed away
Gives somewhere back the thoughts by England
  given;
Her sights and sounds, dreams happy as her days
And laughter, learned at friends, and gentleness,
In hearts at peace, under an English heaven.

Most people today would think that Wilfred Owen's poems on the nature of warfare were more powerful than Brooke's elegiac musings. Yet, it is pretty clear from his letters that Brooke realised the futility of the whole exercise, even though he never fired shot in anger and died of an insect bite, of all things. Owen, on the other hand, never let his feelings interfere with his duty and was killed in almost the last headlong rush into machine gun fire of the war. With terrible cruelty the news only reached his family after the bells had rung to tell the country that peace had finally arrived. While Owen's poems speak to us today about the horror of industrialised warfare, it is Brooke's patriotic lines that are inscribed on the gravestones of British soldiers around the world.

One man who lost his only son in the First World War was Rudyard Kipling. As was common at the time he pulled strings, not to have John excused from combat but to see that he went to war. Poor eyesight could have been used as an excuse to give him a desk job but both father and son worked to send him to the front – with inevitable results. John Kipling's body was never found and his father's patriotism and faith in the system was severely tested by the loss.

John was not the only one of Kipling's three children to die young. One of his daughters died from a fever, one that he had also caught, the news being kept from him in case the grief and shock should tip him over. Kipling is thought of as the poet of the stiff upper lip, the man who celebrated the glories of the British Empire. Some of his writing does lapse into jingoism, but he had a surprisingly light touch at times. My favourite poem of his is The Roman Centurion's Song, which is a little too long to quote in full. The first and last parts of it, however, work well when we stop to see Hadrian's Wall, which is mentioned in the second verse (Vectis is the Isle of Wight):

> Legate I had the news last night - my cohort ordered home
> By ship to Portus Itius and thence by road to Rome.
> I've marched the company aboard, the arms are stored below:
> Now let another take my sword. Command me not to go!
>
> I've served in Britain forty years, from Vectis to the Wall,
> I have none other home than this, nor any life at all
> Last night I did not understand, but now the hour draws near
> That calls me to my native land, I feel that land is here
> Here where my name was made, here where my work was done;
> Here, where my dearest dead are laid - my wife - my wife and son;
> Here where time custom, grief and toil, age, memory, service, love,

*Have rooted me in British soil. Ah, how can I re
  move?*
*For me this land, that sea, these airs, those folk
  and fields suffice.*
*What purple southern pomp can match our
  changeful Northern skies,*
*Black with December's snows unshed, or pearled
  with August haze -*
*The clanging arch of steel grey March, or June's
  long-lighted days?...*
*Legate I come to you in tears - my cohort ordered
  home!*
*I've served in Britain forty years. What should I
  do in Rome?*
*Here is my heart, my soul, my mind, the only life I
  know.*
*I cannot leave it all behind – command me not to
  go!*

There is a hint here of the writer's own loss in the lament of the soldier sent back to a home he can no longer regard as his own. Kipling's own childhood involved being sent from India to England, a miserable experience for him, but he came to love varying patterns of the British countryside, those changeful northern skies.

Kipling's life has certain parallels with that of Shakespeare, who also had three children, lost one to illness when young, saw a daughter marry a man he did not approve of, and whose line died out soon after he did. Like many men who feel they have neglected their children, Shakespeare became obsessively concerned with them in later years. His son Hamnet was dead but there were two daughters: Susannah, who married late, like her mother, but this time to an older man. This union produced a child, another girl, but seems to have been largely platonic afterwards. The other daughter, sad simple Judith, married even later, to a man called Thomas Quiney, who was a local lowlife with a terrible reputation. Their three children died young and Susannah's only daughter also died childless. In Shakespeare's world there were only two ways to cheat death – by writing works that endured and by producing children who continued your line. As his life came to a close he seems to have left the works behind to concentrate on the children. It is sad that, while the works live on, the line died out within a couple of generations.

We probably come closest to Shakespeare the man in his sonnets, the series of a hundred and fifty two poems of fourteen lines that chronicle the relationship between the poet and his patron. Forests have been felled in the cause of identifying the characters concerned but the accepted wisdom is that the poems are addressed to the handsome young aristocrat Henry Wriothesley, Earl of Southampton, and that there may have been an agenda of encouraging the Earl to marry and provide grandchildren for his mother who may have commissioned them at first. The relationship soon developed from one of formal praise and flattery into an intense emotional bond and then decayed as an unknown woman, 'the dark lady' of the sonnets, came between them. While the later poems are tinged with sadness and bitterness, the early ones are full of flattery and not a little showing off, as in the famous sonnet eighteen:

> *Shall I compare thee to a summer's day?*
> *Thou art more lovely and more temperate:*
> *Rough winds do shake the darling buds of May,*
> *And summer's lease hath all too short a date:*
> *Sometime too hot the eye of heaven shines,*
> *And often is his gold complexion dimmed:*
> *And every fair from fair sometime declines*
> *By chance, or nature's changing course*
>   *untrimmed;*
> *But thy eternal summer shall not fade,*
> *Nor lose possession of that fair thou owest,*
> *Nor shall death brag thou wanderest in his shade,*

CHAPTER FOURTEEN

When in eternal lines to time thou growest;
So long as men can breathe and eyes can see,
So long lives this and this gives life to thee.

Shakespeare makes the moral of his sonnets easy by summing up the message in the last two lines of the poem: your beauty and majesty will far outlive the beauty of a mere summer's day as I write poems that will preserve it forever.

Yet for all this concern for the immortality of his verse he seems to have taken very little trouble to ensure that the poems were actually preserved for posterity. The sonnets may well have been published without his consent or co-operation and they remain intensely private in nature. Possibly it was the death of his son and the ending of the male line that made him move his focus back to family matters. We know little of his relationship with Anne Hathaway, but they appear to have learned to live together again reasonably placidly when he returned to Stratford and are buried together in the Holy Trinity church. In his will he left her the famous 'second best bed', which some people take to be an insult, but which was probably a perfectly normal domestic arrangement, the best bed going to guests. The message to his family was surely that his widow should be looked after when he was gone. You can see an older Shakespeare as a contented, prosperous, slightly plump pillar of society in a bust in the church above their grave, one that Anne is reported to have approved of as a good likeness. Only a quill pen indicates that he made his considerable fortune from writing.

Shakespeare's last lines were written on his grave just a few feet from this bust. His epitaph provides a huge contrast to the eloquence of so much of what came before:

Good friend, for Jesu's sake forebear
To dig the dust enclosed here.
Blessed be he who leaves these stones,
And cursed be he who moves my bones.

197

It is hardly inspirational but the message is clear – I want to be left in peace with my family. None of his theatrical friends were at his funeral and he seems to have left the big city behind as he returned home

But let us leave Shakespeare with a piece of late doggerel. Sonnet twenty nine is my personal favourite:

> When in disgrace with fortune and men's eyes,
> I all alone beweep my outcast state,
> And trouble deaf heaven with my bootless cries,
> And look upon myself, and curse my fate,
> Wishing me like to one more rich in hope,
> Featured like him, like him with friends
> possessed,
> Desiring this man's art, and that man's scope,
> With what I most enjoy contented least;
> Yet in these thoughts myself almost despising,
> Haply I think on thee, and then my state,
> Like to the lark at break of dawn arising
> From sullen earth, sings hymns at heaven's gate;
> For thy sweet love such wealth brings
> That then I scorn to change my state with kings.

While Shakespeare is obviously tied mainly to Stratford, he can appear in other places in Britain – in Scotland's Tay Valley where Birnam wood that came to Dunsinane stands, at Bosworth field near Nuneaton where Richard III cried out for a horse, even in the Wye Valley in Wales where Prince Hal was born. There is a statue of him in Monmouth just behind and above the statue of the aviator Charles Rolls in Agincourt Square. (Rolls was the flying half of Rolls Royce.)

The story of Hal and Falstaff is always worth a few minutes as you go from Monmouth to Tintern. Shakespeare may not score highly on accuracy as a historian but he makes up for it with a sense of the truth of the characters he portrays. That wild young man who gets into such scrapes with good John Falstaff knows full well that he will betray and scorn his old friend as the demands of kingship arrive. Sure enough, having taken his dying father's advice, he turns to the old man who is confident in the power of his friendship and then crushes him mercilessly as Falstaff appeals to "my sweet boy":

> *I know thee not, old man: fall to thy prayers;*
> *How ill white hairs become a fool and a jester!*

Although Falstaff never existed outside Shakespeare's imagination, his portrait of the charismatic but chilling Henry is worth a dozen biographies.

Tintern overlaps with the poetry of William Wordsworth, who wrote Lines Composed Above Tintern Abbey, one of the Lyrical Ballads written with his friend and fellow poet Samuel Taylor Coleridge. They were published in 1798 and Romantic Poetry was born. This curious pairing was the Lennon and McCartney of two hundred years ago, the young men of very different temperaments who came together and struck creative sparks off each other. When their temperamental differences led them to drift apart neither created work of such power again. It has been said that Wordsworth was the great poet of sunlight in English, while Coleridge was the great poet of moonlight. Certainly the tall and upright Wordsworth with his devoted wife and sister makes quite a contrast with the restless and drug-addicted Coleridge whose mind and body never settled anywhere for long.

On closer examination, however, it turns out that Wordsworth was not such a saint. He, like many young men of the time, had been filled with enthusiasm for the changes brought about by the French Revolution and had gone to live there for a time. "Bliss was it at that dawn to be alive, but to be young was very heaven!" he wrote in The Prelude, the long autobiographical poem not published until after his death. He had actually set up home with and had a child by an older French woman Annette Vallon but, although he maintained contact with mother and daughter, and even sought Annette's permission to marry Mary Hutchinson, he kept this side of his life secret as he became an increasingly conservative member of the establishment, railing against the tourists who were inspired to visit the Lake District by his poetry.

Dove Cottage, the home Wordsworth shared with his sister Dorothy and later Mary, is one of the literary shrines of Britain, although not many tour parties visit there. Most groups spend an hour or two in the village of Grasmere and sample some of the Kendal Mint Cake available at the shop in the Cumbria Carvery and a few people wander down for a look at the Cottage, where according to Dorothy, they lived a life of "plain living and high thinking", the simple intellectual life they could manage on an income of fifty pounds a year. Later, when things became more comfortable and there were children to support, they moved the few miles down the road to Rydal Mount, also a museum, although the poet, his wife and sister, as well as several other Wordsworth's are buried in the ground's of St Oswald's church in Grasmere.

It was in the next valley, Ullswater, that William and Dorothy saw the daffodils that inspired the famous poem of that name. The poem I quote most often of Wordsworth's, however, is probably his sonnet Upon Westminster Bridge. It is curious but somehow fitting that the greatest poem about London should be written by a man who disliked the city and was hurrying back to his beloved countryside, when he suddenly catches a view of the river in the early morning light:

> *Earth has not anything to show more fair:*
> *Dull would he be of soul who could pass by*
> *A sight so touching in its majesty:*

The city now doth like a garment wear
The beauty of the morning; silent, bare
Ships, towers, domes, theatres and temples lie
Open to the fields and to the sky;
All bright and glittering in the smokeless air.
The sun never did more beautifully steep
In his first splendour, valley, rock or hill;
Never saw I, never felt, a clam so deep!
The river glideth at its own sweet will:
Dear God, the very houses seem asleep;
And all that mighty heart is lying still!

There is only one place to read or recite this poem, actually upon Westminster Bridge.   Other poems can be shifted around depending on the itinerary, the group's attention or the occasion, but somewhere in Scotland you have to touch on the life and work of Robert Burns. Burns was born in 1759, two years after William Blake and just over ten years before Wordsworth. He was another outsider who became a pillar of the establishment towards the end of his life and after his death. Go into almost any town or village in Scotland and sooner or later you will find someone who knows many of his poems off by heart and can tell stories of his various love affairs and the ballads that came out of them. Burns is a hero to the Scots because he spoke and wrote in their language, taught the people to identify with their own culture rather than that of their overbearing neighbours to the south and because he contradicts the image of the dour Scots farmer whose is ever so careful with his money. Any time Robert Burns came into some cash he spent it on those three old favourites – wine, women and song.

The language is difficult to come to terms with. Scots is not a different tongue to English, just a strong dialect version of it. Take the famous first lines of To a Mouse:

Wee, sleekit, cowran, timorous beastie,

O what a panic's in thy breastie!
Thou need na start awe sae hasty
Wi' bickering brattle!
I wad be laith to run and chase thee,
Wi' murdering pattle!

If you do not understand all the words, you can gather through their rhythm that someone is running away here. It is a field mouse whose world has been turned upside down by the plough Burns has been using to turn over the soil in his father's farm. Burns feels sorry for the mouse as it runs away and cries out to him not to be afraid. He does not mean him any harm but, by working the fields to make a living from the land, he sentimentally believes that he has ruined a bond between different species and deprived the mouse of his home and store of food for the winter. As he concludes,

The best- laid schemes o' mice and men
Gang aft agley... (often go wrong).

It is a phrase we often use, reinvented by the American writer John Steinbeck in his story of the little people and their hopes that are crushed by a bigger power.

Another phrase from Burns came from a poem inspired by going to church. Burns was not a naturally pious man but was expected at the kirk, as it was known, on Sundays. One day, dutifully sitting through one of those interminable Presbyterian sermons, he noticed that Jenny, a lady of his acquaintance who was late for church, was sitting in front of him with the finery of her Sunday clothes rather spoilt by a louse climbing up the side of her bonnet. He has an imaginary conversation with the insect:

Ha, where ya gaun, ye crowlan' ferlie?
Your impudence protects you sairly...

The conversation continues as Burns reflects on human

vanity, concluding with the thought that we would be less vain of our appearance if we could see through others eyes:

> *O wad some Power the giftie gie us*
> *To see oursels as others see us!*

This is not life-changing stuff, just down to earth, common sense and humorous reflection. Burns, despite the language difference, lives on in a way that other poets have not because he speaks to ordinary people, particularly those from his own country. There is a huge contrast between the language of the poetry, understood fully by only a few, and the well known phrases, recognised by all. Although he only lived to be thirty seven, Burns left a legion of poems, stories and songs that are remembered in his country and by Scots around the world, particularly on his birthday, 25th January, when they celebrate his life and work.

I cannot attempt a complete literary guide to Britain in one chapter, but I have found these poems and passages help to bring places to life. Others would include Dylan Thomas's Under Milk Wood in Wales, WB Yeats in Ireland, the Bronte sisters in Yorkshire, R D Blackmore's Lorna Doone in and around Exmoor (there is a wonderful description of the aftermath of the battle of Sedgemoor in the chapter Slaughter in the Marshes) and Daphne du Maurier throughout Cornwall. J K Rowling's world is one of the imagination, but you can find Hogwart's in the places where it has been put on film (see chapter twelve) and she will surely be mentioned in Edinburgh where, as a young single mother, she wrote the stories that made her name and fortune.

That is the great thing about guiding - you have no excuse for boredom. There is always another book to read, route to research or subject to study. Who needs hobbies when you a tourist guide?

CHAPTER FIFTEEN:

THEIR UGLY HEADS

Sex, death and race on tour

Bring two guides together and they will pretty soon ask each other, "Do you have a good group?" Various horror stories follow as disasters are recounted and failures remembered. It is one of the saddest things about tourist guiding – you remember the unhappy passenger long after the great majority of satisfied customers have faded from memory. The tours in which people laugh at all the jokes (well, most of them) and seem to be interested and co-operative fly past while the ones in which you struggle to gain a reaction seem to drag on for days rather than hours, months rather than weeks.

Yet there should be no such thing as a bad group or a bad passenger. Perhaps the best analogy is from cricket. The Australian fast bowler Jeff Thomson once described his attempts to chat up a particular type of girl as like bowling on a very slow wicket. It was hard work but the sense of gratification if you achieved a result was all the greater. For the uninitiated a slow wicket is unresponsive and flat, while a fast or quick wicket is lively and unpredictable. Bowlers tend to be successful on quick wickets, batsmen on slower ones. Tour guides prefer quick wickets, responsive groups who seem to be lively and interested, but these parties can be unpredictable and suddenly turn against you if something goes wrong. Slow wicket groups are harder work when it comes to eliciting a response but, with careful handling, are less likely to blow up when things go wrong – and winning them over is that much more satisfying.

Everyone who spends the time and money to buy a tour starts with a degree of enthusiasm for the project but some lose it more quickly than others. No-one actually buys a tour thinking in advance how much fun they can have by complaining about the problems they encounter. Some are quicker to spot problems than others just as some are quicker to express enthusiasm. Women are generally more enthusiastic than men while, perhaps surprisingly, an older group is more likely to provide a guide with a quick wicket than a younger one. Teenagers, in particular, are too worried about looking cool in front of their peers to show any interest in the dumb stories of some tour guide.

Some nationalities also tend to be livelier than others. Overseas groups are usually more boisterous than British ones – people have fewer inhibitions away from home. American parties are famous for their willingness to join in the fun and make lots of noise. This can become embarrassing at times. One passenger was so interested in the field of small wooden memorial crosses next to Westminster Abbey when we were visiting there just before poppy day that he helped himself to one and had to be politely but firmly told to put it back.

Israeli groups have a reputation for being enormously demanding, while parties from the Commonwealth are, like their British ancestors, more phlegmatic, willing to grin and bear it if there are any problems - as long as their national identity is acknowledged. Never confuse a New Zealander with an Australian or a Canadian with someone from the USA. People from the Far Eastern countries are travelling to Britain increasingly these days. Although their English is usually excellent it is a second language for them and their cultural references are totally different. Inevitably their sense of humour and interest in history is different to that of people from a more Anglo-Saxon background and it is harder to work up a response from them. Don't try to tell a joke to a group from the Far East if it involves any complicated punning or British assumptions. Rather spend some time coming to grips with their curious three pronged names.

Inscrutable Orientals, noisy Americans, demanding Israelis and down to earth Australians? We are skirting dangerously close to racism here. Although racism should have no part in tourism, national stereotyping inevitably drifts in. This can slide into racism almost imperceptibly without anyone intending it. People come to Britain to experience a golden era of thatched cottages, friendly neighbours and tight knit communities, the world portrayed so successfully by James Herriot. This is a mono-racial world where black people have not exactly been excluded, but neither have they been welcomed in. The fact is that there are few black faces in tour groups, in tour guide training courses and in tour company brochures. No-one intended this but it is an area where we are behind other industries in coming into the twenty first century – probably because we spend so much time in previous eras.

The only time I might actually introduce the subject of racism to a tour is if I talk about slavery. There is a statue of John Colston in the city centre of Bristol. He was a philanthropist and benefactor of the poor, although his statue makes him seem like a thoroughly miserable character. Maybe he had a guilty conscience because his money came from slavery. The statue of William Wilberforce in Westminster Abbey, however, shows a marvellously determined and prickly man. I always point it out and tell people that he was a pioneer of the abolition of slavery. The bill to abolish the slave trade was introduced by Charles James Fox shortly before his death and the memorial in the Abbey commemorating Fox shows a suitably grateful Negro in chains offering thanks at Fox's feet. He, the only black man represented in the Abbey, is of course anonymous. He has become part of our heritage rather than an individual.

In truth racism rarely rears its ugly head on tours, while sex and death rear theirs every so often. There is always money to be made from man's inhumanity to man and a sub genre of Dungeon museums and displays does respectable business by appealing to bloodthirsty young males who also buy history books 'without the boring bits' in them. I should not sneer. I have used the gruesome death of William Wallace a few times on tour to grab people's attention when introducing Scotland's fight for independence which culminated in victory at Bannockburn for Robert the Bruce in 1314. This is the one part of the film Braveheart that was reasonably accurate, the rest being a mishmash of fantasy and exaggeration, ironically filmed largely in Ireland (for tax reasons). In particular, the sex element introduced into the later part of the film is laughable. The idea that William Wallace had a relationship with Isabella, the princess who was married to Edward II, and that he was the real father of the prince who became Edward III was pretty unlikely even before you consider that Wallace was executed in 1305 and Edward III was not born until 1312. Even Mel Gibson could not make a woman pregnant for seven years.

This kind of violence and sexual fantasy is acceptable in a story seven or eight centuries old but becomes more uncomfortable the closer to home you get. Braveheart may have boosted the Scottish tourist economy but any hint of violence from modern terrorists or street criminals has the opposite effect. Occasionally people do say to me, "Eddie, we haven't seen any bad areas yet", to which the only reply is that we tend to avoid them deliberately. I live in Brixton and might take people through there on the way to or from Gatwick airport, but otherwise it has little chance of appearing on any itinerary I am likely to conduct. People are more interested in seeing a quaint village on a Sunday morning rather than an inner city on a Saturday night. Occasionally the real world imposes itself if you are staying in an urban area and a group of drunks starts behaving badly. This is a depressingly common possibility in even small towns in Britain and soon cures people of the desire to see the worse parts of the country.

Even without evidence of the inability of British youth to hold its drink, people used to a quiet life can be disoriented and frightened by the experience of modern travel. As I have indicated (all guides repeat the important things at least once) they need a friendly and sensitive individual who shows some enthusiasm for his work to identify with. The best qualified guide soon learns that he has to give something of himself to his work, something more than just his knowledge. The sensible one keeps something behind for his family and friends. One of the reasons for the high failure rate in marriages and relationships in the guiding and tour directing community is that successful guides give *too* much of themselves to their passengers and not enough to their loved ones.

Another reason is that there are plenty of temptations on tour. Drivers, guides and tourists away from home slip into impulsive night time behaviour which can seem pretty silly in the morning. Most companies did not concern themselves with this for years but a tendency amongst passengers to telephone their lawyers when they get home has produced a change of climate. I had a second hand taste of this when I organised a ride on the jaunting carts in Killarney. Two middle-aged American women convinced themselves that their Irish driver's light-hearted comments on their beauty and his need for a good wife constituted sexual harassment. I became answerable for his behaviour and he was banned for a season from taking our people for, I suppose, a ride. He had made these corny comments before (and, I am sure, since) and most people enjoyed them, but two offended people with no-win no-fee lawyers behind them can do a good deal of damage.

Unlike sex, death cannot be avoided. I have never actually 'lost' anyone on a tour in this way – although some people have looked pretty comatose when I start talking about the dissolution of the monasteries. It is every guide's nightmare: everything seems to be going well and then someone suddenly dies. The atmosphere, from being jovial and optimistic, suddenly turns cold. It would be fair to say that most of the people in a tour group have more of their lives behind them than in front of them and, for many, a tour is something they have saved up for to enjoy in retirement when they can slow down. They had not anticipated stopping, however, and what seemed like a life-affirming experience becomes a reminder to people of their mortality.

It takes some time to recover from the death of a passenger or their departure from the tour due to illness, but recovery is possible. Remember the analogy of the quick and the slow wicket. A lively group can turn around very quickly into a vociferous one, while a quiet group can be won over by patience and tact. Every 'bad' event has the potential to make the guide look good. Some guides even like to build in their mistakes so that they can make light of them and show their human side. Others do not need to rehearse disasters. (They come naturally to us.) It is how we deal with the difficulties that people judge us. Prompt and sensitive handling of a difficult situation can win the guide great kudos with his group so no event needs to turn out wholly bad. One of my best memories is not of a passenger but of a coach dying on me. We had a great time as I organised taxis and found an ancient school bus and equally ancient driver as replacements. We arrived at out hotel at around eight o'clock, just in time for the last sitting at dinner.

Similarly, one of my most difficult and cantankerous passengers found that her mother was gravely ill while we were on tour. I told her that there was a message for her and left her to decide what to do. She decided to return and we simply took her to the airport on the way out of Edinburgh the next day (it was on the way, sort of). While I was not heartbroken to see the back of her, just the lift to the airport seemed to win her over before we parted company. To be fair to her, this was her second or third tour in succession and I think that no-one had extended any simple act of consideration like this in the month or two she had been away from home.

No-one can predict when a death will occur, although it is obviously closer for some than others. Occasionally a guide will push his passengers too hard when they simply want some time to relax, to sleep or, to use the modern phrase, to chill. I have felt this both as a guide and a tourist.

On one particular run, we arrive in Dublin after a long journey across Ireland. I have told them about the famine, the religious wars, the division of the country between 1916 and 1922 and about the leprechauns. We are staying at the Gresham hotel in the centre of Dublin, where they can easily find a hamburger or fish and chips around the corner, and it seems best *not* to organise anything for the group but to leave them to their own devices. I wash my socks and go to the cinema next door or, if I have the energy, to the Abbey theatre down the road. Next morning we convene to look at the city after a late breakfast and everybody seems better for the break.

Occasionally I like to fool myself that the reason I have never had a death is because I do not push people too hard. I insist on setting aside and highlighting certain times like this when the group (and the guide) are left to themselves and, whenever possible, I try to allow people to return to their hotel rooms if they do not want to shop or visit another museum in their free time. Out of town hotels are often used by tour companies because they are cheaper than city centre ones, but this can mean that people's free time is spent wandering around a big and crowded city, which can be even more stressful than sitting on the coach, where they can at least have a nap. Many people do not take the option of returning to the hotel, but sometimes even the most motivated and enthusiastic tourist needs time to recharge.

However it is caused, if a death comes, the guide should not jump to any conclusions. First of all, a passenger is not dead until a doctor says so. A guide should never show up at a hospital saying that one of his passengers has died, even if he has not moved for hours and is missing several essential elements. Hospitals are for the living – undertakers are for the dead. Undertakers expect payment, hospitals do not (usually) charge for their services. At hospitals, you can hand over the sick and leave them to get on with their job, maintaining contact by telephone. At an undertaker, you will need to make complicated and time-consuming arrangements on the spot while your group is left leaderless.

A tour director I met worked on cruise ships occasionally and he said that body preservation was a big issue there. They would have a doctor on board who could pronounce on death, but it was bad policy to bury the client at sea. It smacked of a cover-up and people are quick to sue on suspicion in the hope of a quick settlement. What they did was to store the body in the ice-making room. There is plenty of drinking on cruises and people like ice in their cocktails, so they just made a little extra room there to avoid the twin problems of decomposition or disposal.

Another guide was a trained nurse and used to dealing with the elderly and sick. On the way to the airport, one of her passengers passed away quietly. She realised what had happened and wrapped the passenger in a coat, saying that he was merely sleeping. Strictly speaking, she should have stopped the coach and summoned medical assistance as soon as possible, but this would have almost certainly meant the entire group missing their flight so she told the driver to continue to the airport, where the group could check in while she took care of the already departed.

This was surely the best thing to do at the time, but it was a high risk strategy. The guide should always see that sick passengers are given medical treatment as soon as possible. This generally means bringing a doctor to the sick, but there might be times when you can get to the doctor more easily. Most guides are trained in first aid these days, but there is a limit to what can be done by the amateur and people are quick to sue if someone goes beyond his competency. Professional help is best and needs to be arranged as quickly as possible. The passenger should be informed that payment may need to be made and how much it will be. Nowadays there will be little change from £100 if a doctor visits a hotel, even if the consultation only takes five minutes. Tourists can avoid this charge by making use of the National Health Service, but this will usually involve going to a hospital and possibly having a long wait in a crowded and possibly bloody casualty department. Most people are covered by medical insurance and prefer to pay and reclaim.

Sometimes the sick passenger has to be left behind, even though they may wish to continue on the tour. I had a persistent smoker on one tour who would light up at every opportunity – much to the annoyance of other passengers. She reached as far as Limerick where breathing became so difficult that we had to leave her and her husband behind at the hospital. The tour goes on even if some passengers do not and the tour company then becomes responsible for the castaway. She suddenly became more popular once she had left and people missed her jovially defiant smoking. I suspect that my record of never having lost a passenger was very nearly broken on that tour.

Probably the closest I came to losing someone to death was on the Isle of Skye soon after I began taking extended tours around Britain. It was a large group from New Jersey and we were travelling through Scotland. Inevitably the story of Bonnie Prince Charlie and his flight from the redcoats aided by the plucky Flora MacDonald came up. We stopped at Flora's grave at the north end of Skye and then headed thankfully for the hotel at the end of a long day. Suddenly the youngest child in the group started screaming hysterically. He father, sitting next to her, had gone grey. He was a diabetic and something had gone wrong with his blood sugar levels. His wife started to look for his medicine and realised that it was in her suitcase. Fifty six suitcases were unloaded and we found hers. (Why she did not have it in her handbag was one of those unasked or answered questions.) He, still unconscious, was given some medicine and we proceeded to the nearby hotel where I called the local doctor. He arrived promptly, checked the passenger over, gave him a mild sedative by injection and left.

Now, all that this old-fashioned highland doctor would accept in the way of payment was a signature from the patient's wife to indicate that treatment had been carried out. He told me that, in the scattered communities of the

Highlands, it was often necessary to visit isolated people and that he could reclaim the expenses easily through the local health board. The patient's wife was flabbergasted. She simply could not believe that a doctor would visit a patient without charging for his services. And the patient? He woke up the next morning thinking that he had merely fallen asleep and had no idea that there had been a crisis. At least it was a good advert for the National Health Service.

However much we praise the NHS, guides and tour directors will never enjoy the job security of working in the public sector. We are essentially freelance and, in the case of accusations of sexual harassment have few rights. A public sector worker accused of impropriety may be suspended pending an inquiry but, theoretically at least, this does not involve a prejudgement of his guilt or innocence. In tourism, however, if you overdo the charm you could be out. For a freelance there is no effective distinction between suspension and dismissal. If you are not offered work because of a complaint made against you, then you do not earn, whatever justification there is behind the complaint. Due process of law is impossible if there are thousands of miles between accused and accuser and only the word of both parties to go on. In sexual matters, many men find that they are effectively guilty until proven innocent. It is best to be above suspicion – or extremely discreet.

However, for every complaint of sexual harassment, there are probably dozens of occasions when some charmer has been given a simple brush off. One mature and attractive lady, who had certainly been a beauty in her youth, wrote to me about her European tour after she had returned home. She told me how their Italian driver had made eyes at her everyday until he got the message and turned his attentions elsewhere. She thought it was more hilarious than flattering and would not have dreamt of contacting a lawyer or writing a formal letter to the company. She may have been secretly pleased at the attention, but there was no chance of anything coming of it – particularly as she was travelling with her elderly mother and had a husband and family to return to.

The Italian driver probably thought it was worth the trouble. He may have scored a blank on that occasion but there would have been successes on other tours. Spouses and families can be forgotten if they are back at home and persistence has its rewards for those who do not mind the odd brush off. What has changed recently is that it also has its penalties. There is a fine line between making it clear that you are interested and being a pest. Some women like a man to show persistence so that they are not perceived as being too easy, while others do not like to show the kind of rudeness you need to get rid of the man who is too full of his himself. A monogamous and mature housewife from the suburbs might be interested in a little fling while she is away, but she may just not have the artillery to deal with a persistent flirt because she has been out of that scene for so long, or never interested in it in the first place. It is now up to the man to read the signals correctly and pay the penalty if he does not.

This is not to say that sex never occurs on tours. Sometimes a minor fling can turn into a major relationship and people leave wives and partners to set up a new life abroad. Almost all these cross-continent relationships are short-lived. A driver or guide can be king of the road for a week or two but, moving to a new country without any relevant skills, he finds himself floundering in the shadow of a new girlfriend who has her own life to lead. The regular routine of early starts, days in the coach and evenings at the bar turns into a long winter of idleness. People who were infatuated with the excitement of a new relationship find they have little in common, friends and children are hostile or indifferent to the new relationship and the runaway returns from his adventure sadder and wiser. If he is lucky his previous partner allows him home once again (never twice).

Guides are best advised to talk about sex rather than practice it. Inevitably it comes into stories and jokes, but this is one of those areas where the guide has to weigh up the group before committing himself to a story. One of my old standbys, the story of how Jimmy got those leads from his priest (see No Laughing Matter) usually goes down well with a group that includes Catholics who, whatever else you think of them, generally have a sense of humour. It went down like a lead balloon with a bunch of Methodists, otherwise a super crowd. Children may be more sexually aware these days than they were a generation or two ago, but it is not a good idea to tell jokes with a sexual element if they are in a group – not because they will necessarily be shocked, but because their parents will. The joke about the two golfers and their wives is safe enough, but nothing stronger.

Sex is, in any case, one of those things you can dance around. Nobody wants specifics but the odd mention of it can grab people's attention. One tour director, who was married to a sheep farmer, used to wake up her groups by saying that it was time to talk about the sex life of sheep. It is not the most interesting topic in the world, but there is a certain novelty there, particularly as most farm animals have no sex life to speak of. We live in an age of factory farming where most breeding is done through artificial insemination. A few males have the demanding job of producing buckets of high class sperm which is then frozen and inserted into as many females as possible, none of whom is allowed any pleasure from the process. Several months later highly engineered offspring are born which are then either castrated (male) and soon slaughtered or set aside for further breeding and milking (female).

The whole process is actually very joyless and scientific but the sheep, for the time being at least, are allowed some pleasure from it. The male sheep still mostly undergo castration soon after birth and their body weight is built up as they become what are known as fat lambs. By law a lamb has to be no more than a year old at slaughter (older than that it is mutton) so the chance of seeing your first birthday if you are born as a male sheep is about one in fifty.

These are the rams who are expected to cover around fifty ewes in the course of quite a short time. The gestation period for sheep is five months less five days and so the rutting, as it is known, takes place in the autumn so the new lambs can be born again in the spring. Sheep are one of the few farm animals left largely free to roam for food in the fields or on the hills, so this cycle ties in with the seasons and has been largely unchanged for centuries. Sheep, sadly, are being dragged into the era of modern farming technology and many Australian sheep are born from artificial insemination these days.

The extent of human ingenuity in British sheep-breeding has not gone beyond the crayon. This is a bag of dye strapped to the ram's belly, some of which rubs onto the fleece of the ewe. This gives important breeding information to farmers as they can tell which ewes have been covered by which rams and this will in turn indicate if certain rams are no longer fertile. Telling this story I like to cross reference sex and death by saying that, if the crayon tells the farmer that one of his rams is no longer producing the goods, off he goes to become mutton stew and another one is brought into service.

The sex life of sheep, which I have learnt from my colleague and from visiting various farms and shepherds, has enlivened a few trips to the Lake District before we move on to Wordsworth and Coleridge. I dropped the line into my commentary a few years ago and one of the female passengers sitting at the front said she knew plenty about this particular subject. I asked her about this later on when we had a break in Grasmere and half-expected the usual reminiscences about being brought up on the family farm. Something about her, however, did not seem like the typical farmer's daughter. It turned out she was a sexual counsellor from San Francisco (where else?) and gave help to people with sexual identity problems. Some of her clients' predilections involved having sex with animals and sheep, apparently, make the best partners for those with that kind of taste: right height and shape and sufficiently pliable not to object, I suppose. We did not cover the topic in detail but did laugh about the different interpretation of the phrase 'sex life of sheep'. I told the story to a few colleagues and friends but it has never worked its way into my commentary. Some things are just too specific.

Of course, reading this kind of book, people expect a certain amount of personal specifics, i.e. descriptions and reminiscences of sexual adventures in life as a tour guide. So are we having going to have any?

Now, about those sheep…

FURTHER CONTACTS

Inevitably some people reading this book may be interested in working in tourism. Be warned, however. Tourist guiding is an overcrowded profession and tour directing (accompanying groups on longer tours) is a notoriously uncertain one. Entering guiding involves taking a course and passing examinations approved by the Institute of Tourist Guiding. Potential guides might not even recoup the cost of the course and exams if work is scarce when they qualify.

Many tour directors have experience in other areas of tourism before they take on an extended tour, either as drivers, guides or holiday reps. Others are just good bluffers and fast learners. Whatever your background, once you have been given a tour you are on continuous trial. Your passengers will decide whether they think you are the right sort of person to run it and there is no appeal against their judgement. A satisfied customer is the best advertisement for a tour company. So, don't mess up your first tour – you might not get second one.

The following organisations are useful for guides and tour directors:

The Institute of Tourist Guiding   Lloyds Court, 1 Goodman's Yard, London E1 8AT (www.itg.org.uk)

The Association of Professional Tourist Guides 33-37 Moreland Street, London EC1V 8HA (www.aptg.org.uk)

The Guild of Registered Tourist Guides   Guild House, 52d Borough High Street, London SE1 1XN (www.blue-badge.org.uk)

International Association of Tour Managers 397

Walworth Road, London SE17 2AW (www.iatm.co.uk)

Scottish Tourist Guides Association Old Town Jail, St John Street, Stirling, FK8 1EA (www.stga.co.uk)

If you are interested in training to be a blue badge guide in London you should start at the website: www.guidetraining. co.uk

If you are interested in booking a guide for a tour, there are several agencies you can use. **Tour Guides Limited**, 57 Duke Street, London, W1K 5NR, (www.tourguides.co.uk or telephone 020 7495 5504) is probably the best one. It also happens to be the one I am a member of.

Printed in the United Kingdom
by Lightning Source UK Ltd.
103991UKS00001B/82-282